I0511523

Romans 1:20

For since the creation of the world God's invisible qualities—his eternal power and divine nature—have been clearly seen, being understood from what has been made, so that people are without excuse.

Author & Photographer Joshua McBride

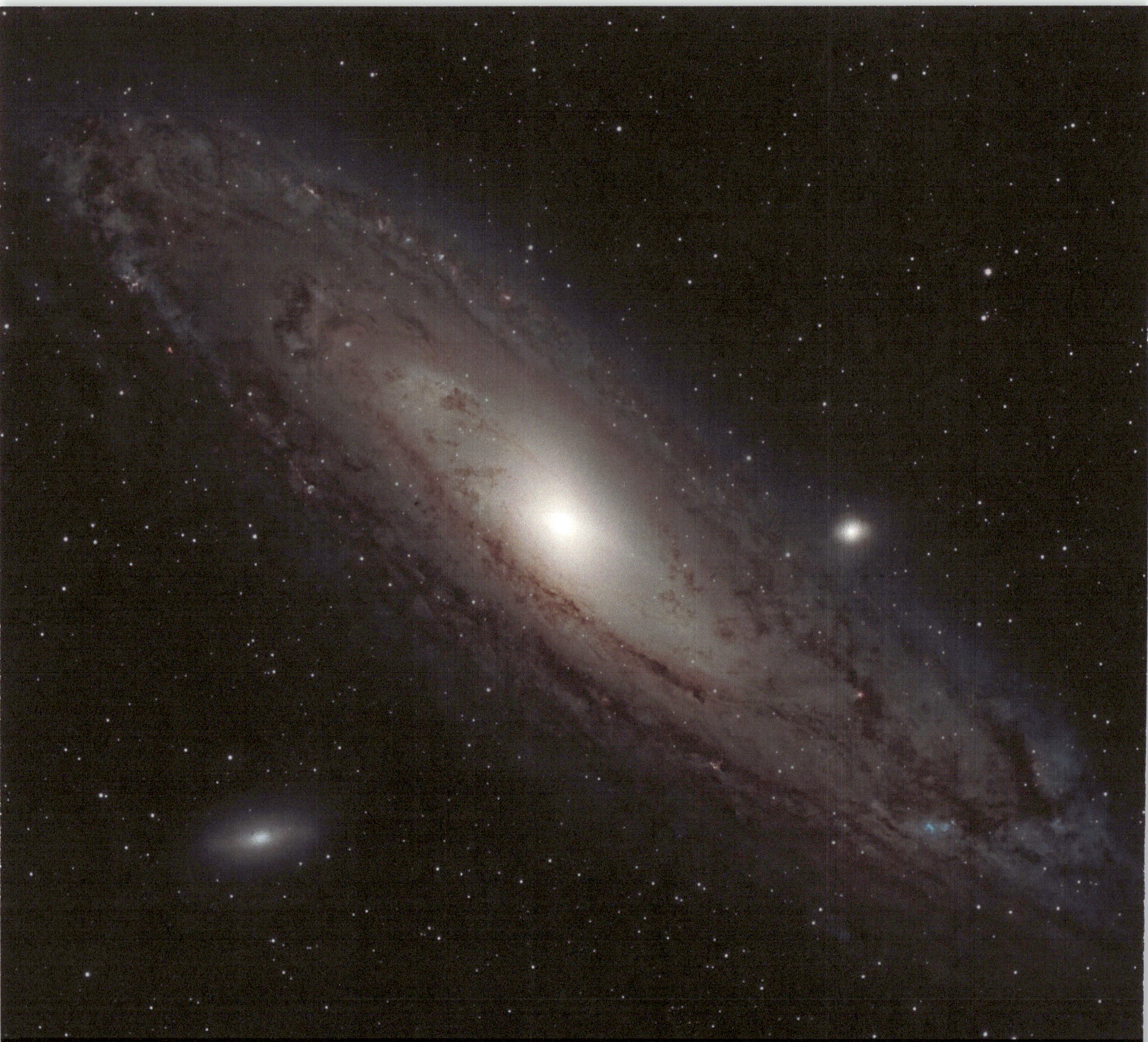

ANDROMEDA

M31

Psalms 68:34

Proclaim the power of God, whose majesty is over Israel, whose power is in the heavens.

Science and Thoughts

The Andromeda Galaxy is the closest galaxy to our own Milky Way Galaxy. It has two satellite galaxies with it as well. It can be seen with the unaided eye viewed from sufficiently dark skies. By assuming standardized star sizes, the galaxy is believed to be 2.5 million light years away. Its vastness can't be grasped by our feeble minds, yet it is nothing compared to God's power!

Image Info

469 x 120 sec images total
Total integration time of **15:38 hours**
Celestron SCT 6"/1500 mm 6 SCT
ZWO Optical ASI183MC Pro (CMOS)
Equatorial iOptron CEM25P
Antlia Contrast booster Quad Band
Astronomik L-1 UV-IR Blocking Filter
Focal reducer Starizona Hyperstar F2

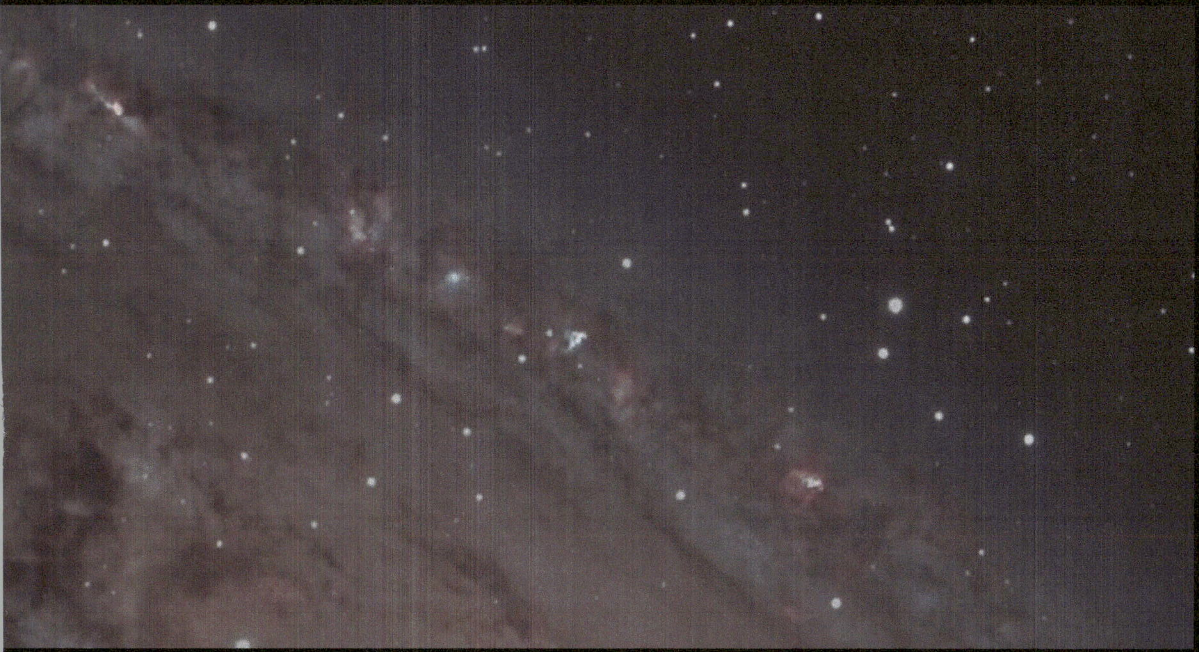

Hydrogen Alpha Nebula

In numerous areas of the galaxy, red nebulas can be seen. These nebulas are composed of Hydrogen thus producing the red color. They illustrate the large amount of activity present in the galaxy as they emit their light as an ionized plasma and are called emission nebulas as a result. They are typically associated with white hot stars at their center.

Dark Lanes

The dark areas seen throughout the galaxy are regions of relatively dense interstellar dust that obscure our view of the stars and other celestial objects behind them. These dark lanes not only make for a more interesting appearance but also help us trace the movement throughout the galaxy as well.

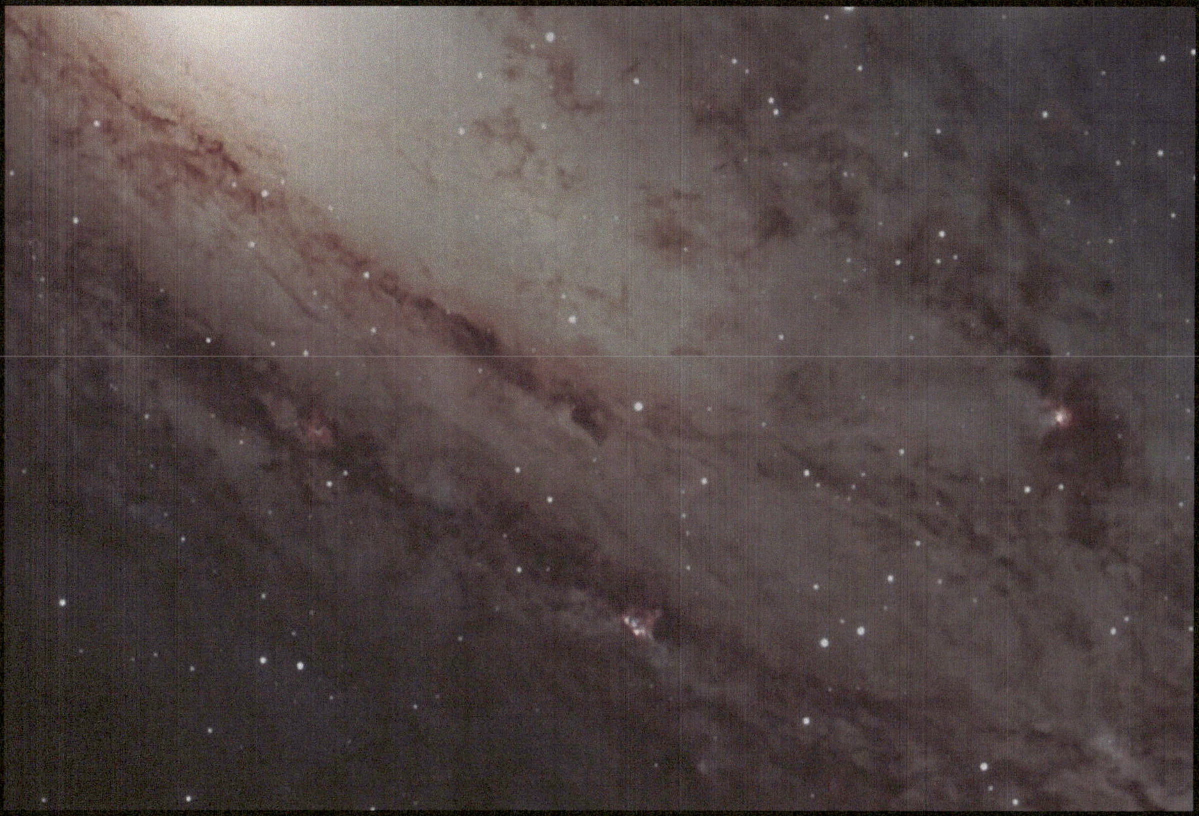

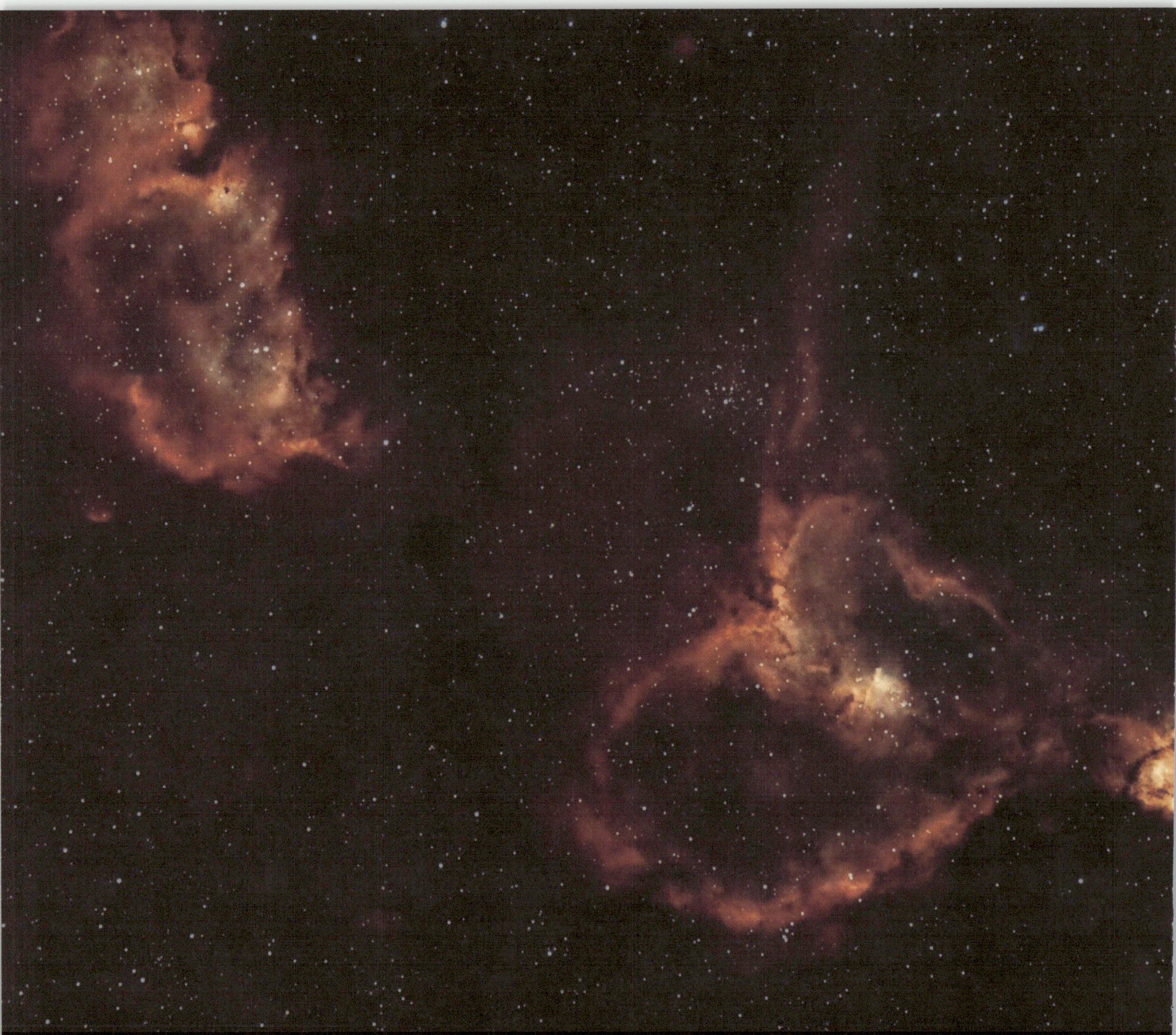

HEART AND SOUL NEBULA

IC 1805 AND IC 1848

Genesis 2:7

Then the LORD God formed a man from the dust of the ground and breathed into his nostrils the breath of life, and the man became a living being.

Science and Thoughts

This massive nebula in our own galaxy is hydrogen plasma. From our perspective the heart alone is 4 times the diameter of the moon. The Soul Nebula looks like a child developing in the womb. Together they are like a giant message, for those who seek Him, reminding us of God's love for his children.

Image Info

147 x 45 sec images total
Total integration time of 1:50 hours
Rokinon Lens 135 mm F2
Sony A6000 (CMOS) - modified
Equatorial iOptron Skyguider Pro
SVBONY Broadband UHC Filter

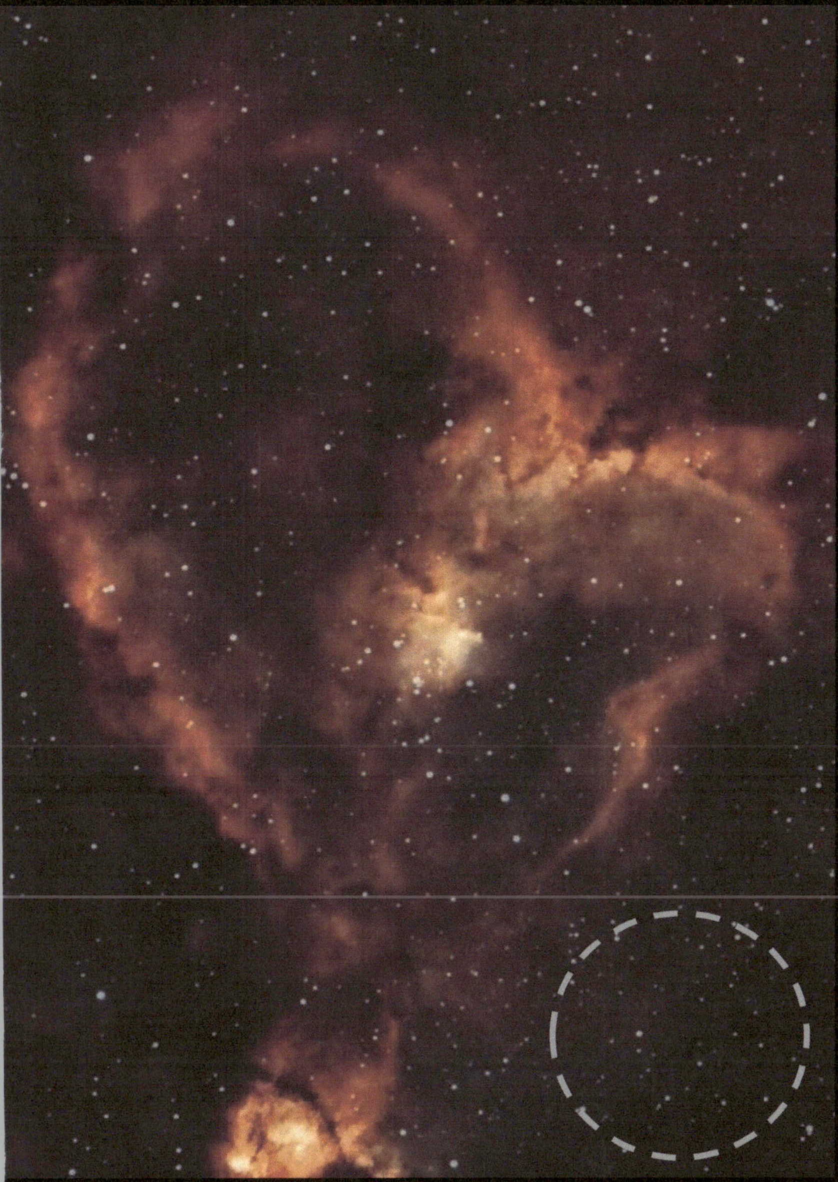

Relative Size to Moon

Located within the Milky Way galaxy, assuming a fixed light speed of 186,000 miles per second, the heart nebula is approximately 200+ light years across and 7,500 light years away. This massive nebula has a relative size, as viewed from earth, of 4 times the diameter of the moon. Pictured to the left, the dashed circle shows the relative size of the moon as compared to the heart nebula.

Massive Stars

At the center of the heart nebula lies a cluster of stars. This cluster contains some stars that appear to be approximately 10 times the diameter of our sun.

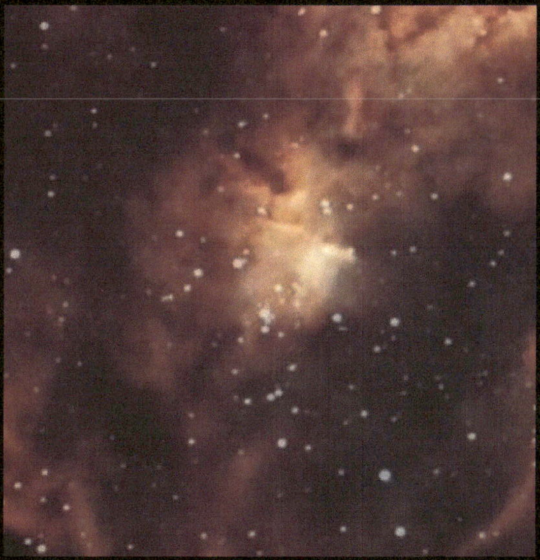

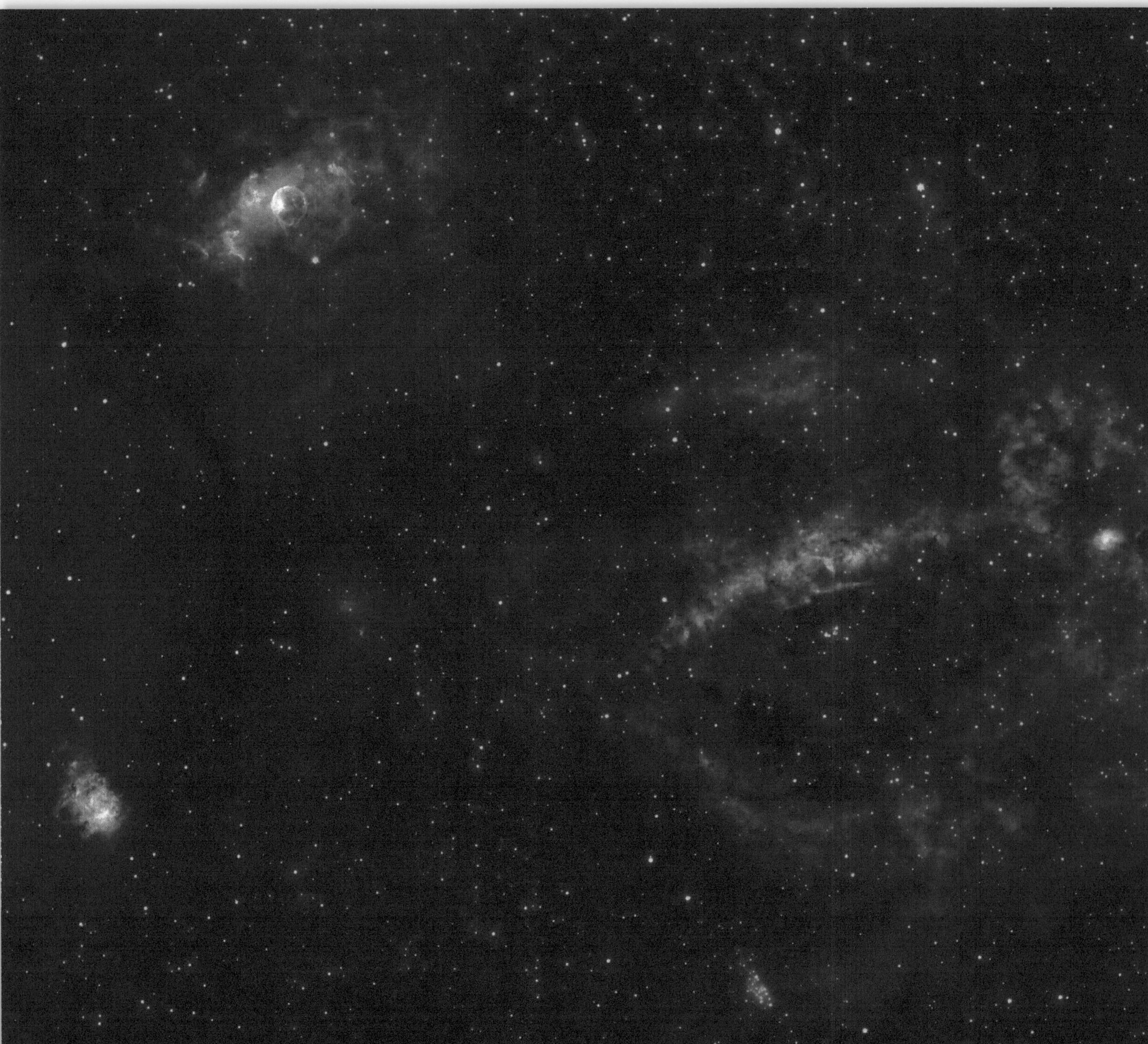

LOBSTER CLAW & BUBBLE NEBULA

SH 1-109 AND NGC 7635

Isaiah 41:13

For I am the LORD your God who takes hold of your right hand and says to you, Do not fear; I will help you.

Science and Thoughts

Another massive nebula of plasma in red (hydrogen) and green/blue (oxygen) can be seen here. Two of the key elements needed for life create the image of a hand reaching across the cosmos. The immense energy in this 320 light year diameter structure is like the hand of God that leads us and protects us.

Image Info

440 x 120 sec images total
Total integration time of 14:40 hours
Celestron SCT 6"/1500 mm 6 SCT
ZWO Optical ASI183MC Pro (CMOS)
Equatorial iOptron CEM25P
Antlia Contrast booster Quad Band
Astronomik L-1 UV-IR Blocking Filter

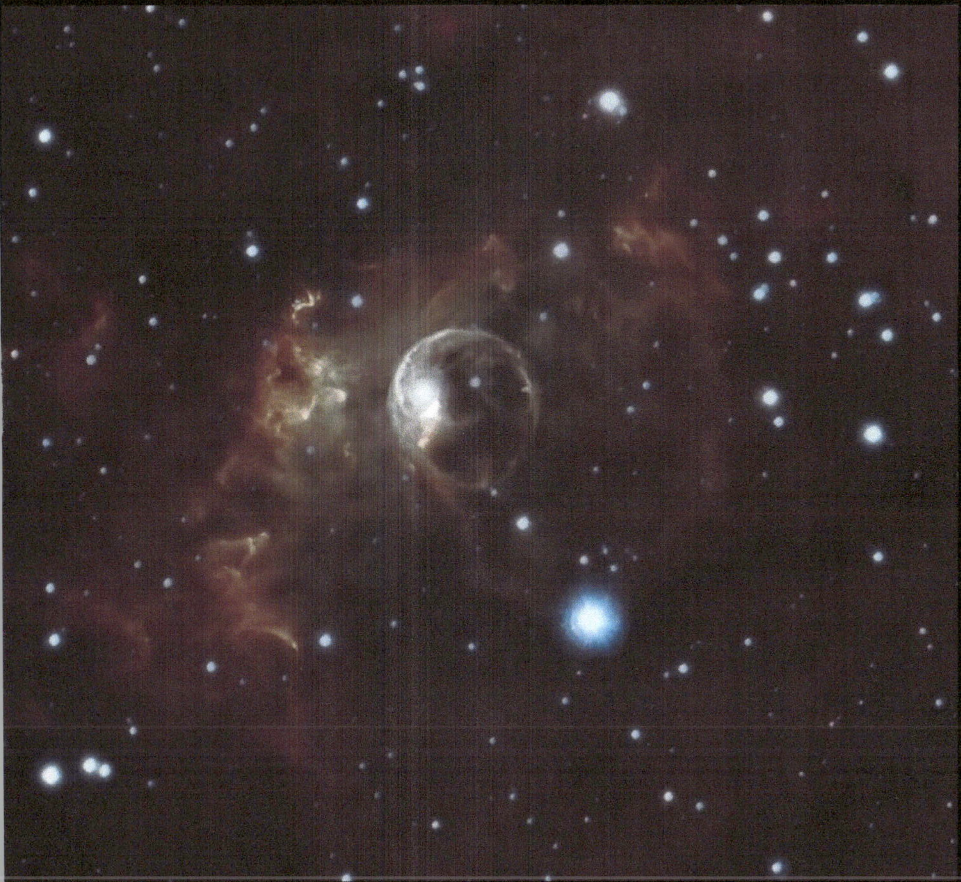

Space Bubble

This bubble of glowing plasma is believed to be caused by the stellar winds of the star at its center interacting with the surrounding gas and dust. These structures are typical in plasmas as Langmuir sheaths or double-layers. The Voyager 1 spacecraft crossed the sun's boundary leaving the heliosphere it become the first man made object to reach interstellar space.

Star Cluster

Near the Lobster Claw Nebula is the star cluster NGC 7510 seen near the bottom of this image. A star cluster is a group of stars that are close enough to be interacting with each other and possibly formed from the same molecular cloud. Much of the light from this cluster is absorbed by interstellar gas and dust. By viewing it in other frequencies of the electromagnetic spectrum such as ultraviolet and infrared, we are able to clearly see the many objects through the dust.

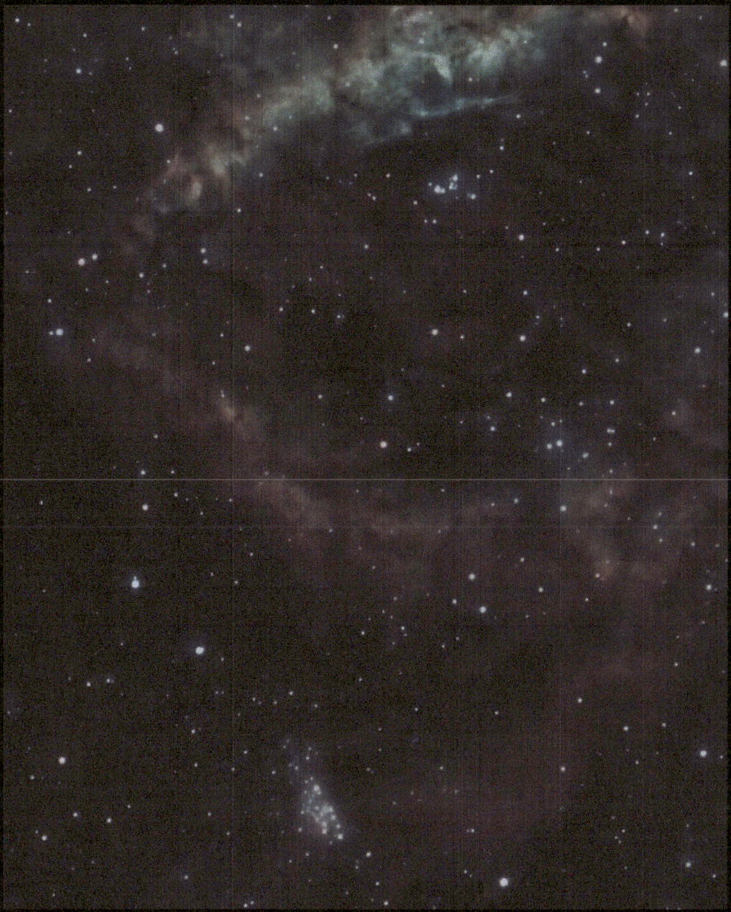

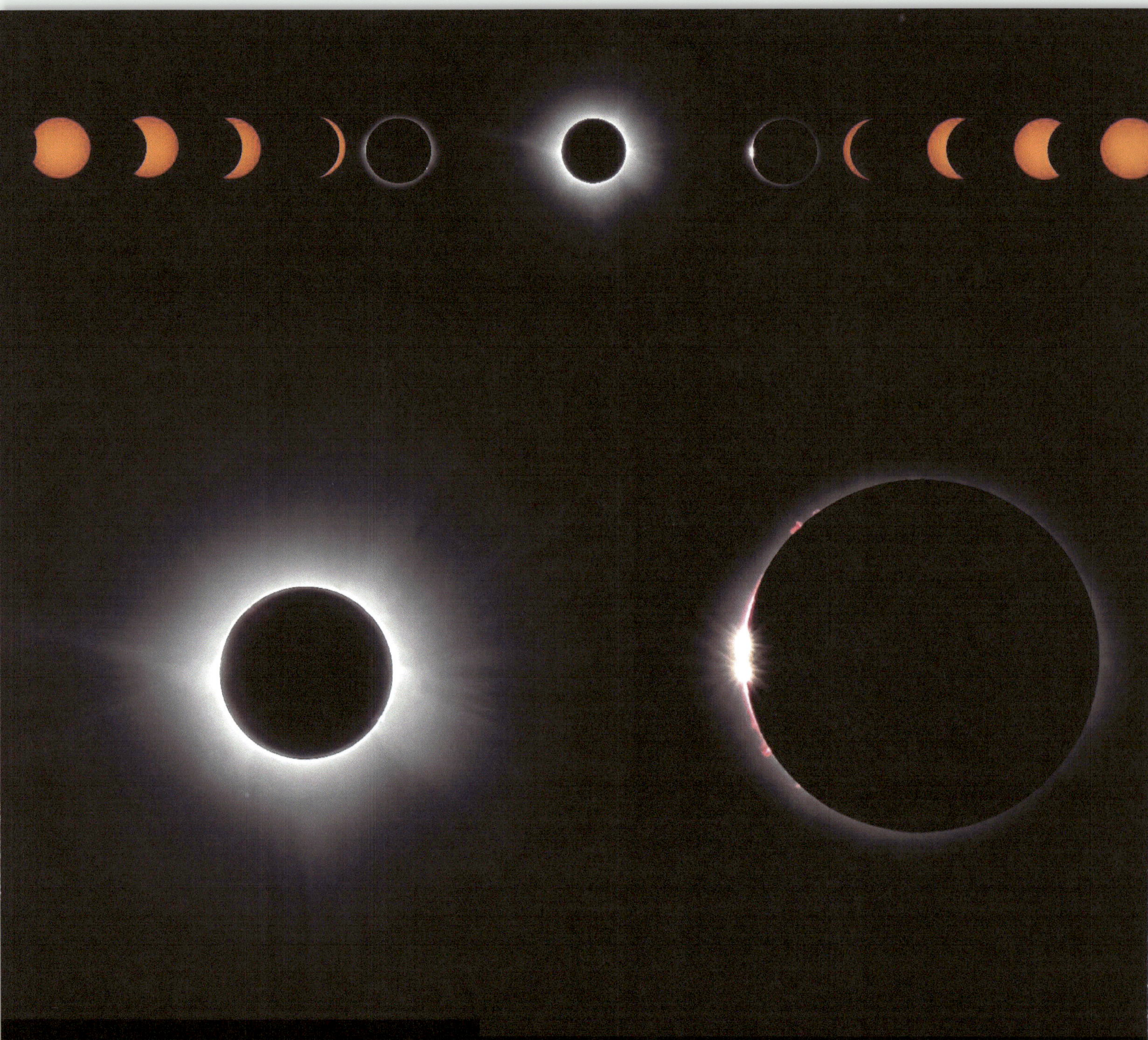

TOTAL SOLAR ECLIPSE

Psalms 34:5
Those who look to him are radiant; their faces are never covered with shame..

Science and Thoughts
This rare celestial event is the only way for us to view the sun's radiant corona with our own eyes. Due to the moon's elliptical orbit, the moon must pass in front of the sun during the closer part of its orbit. Without this special event we cannot see the corona. Without the Son we cannot see the Father.

Image Info
Collection of images
Tokina Lens 300 mm F2.8
Sony A6000 (CMOS) - modified
Equatorial iOptron Skyguider Pro
Thousand Oaks Optical Solar Film

Bailey's Beads

During the eclipse, just as the moon begins to completely cover or uncover the sun, bright 'beads' appear. This is where small parts of the sun's surface appears through 'cracks' between craters and other forms of rough topography along the rim of the moon. Additionally, you can see the solar prominences of plasma leaping up from the surface of the sun and back.

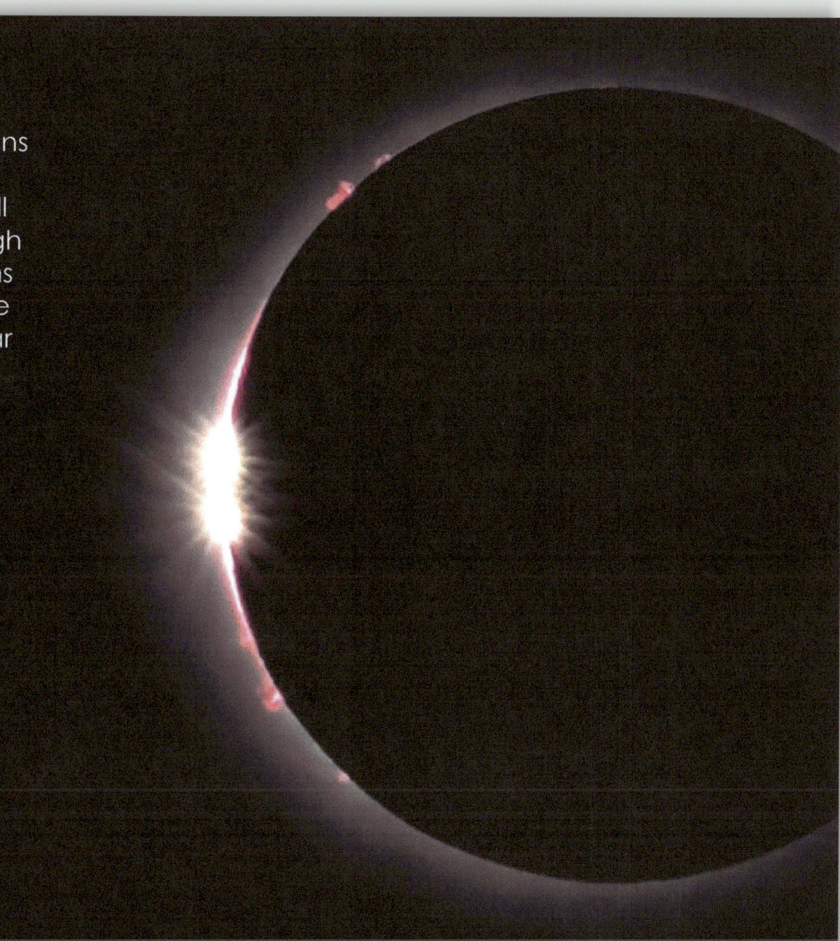

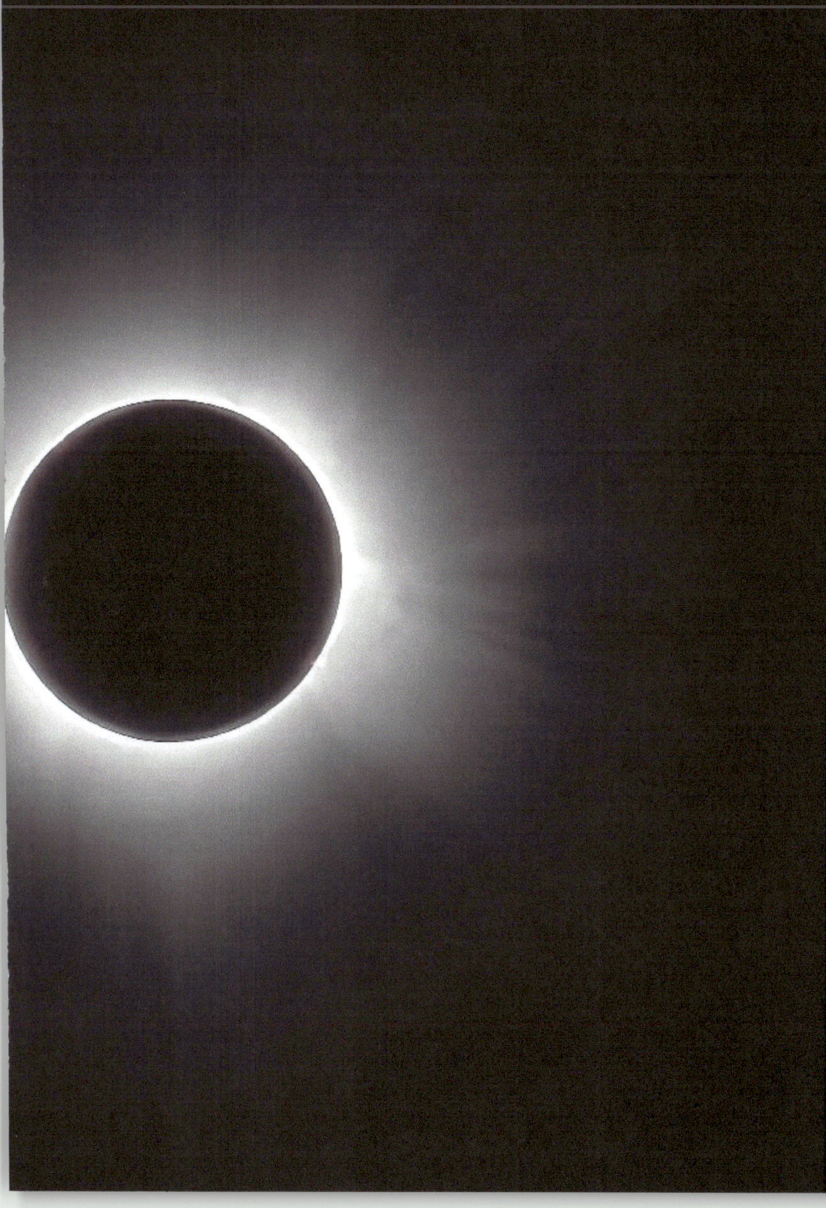

Hydrogen and Plasma

Our understanding of our nearest star, the sun, continues to change and the rare chance to observe the corona is a great opportunity. As seen in the image, plasma streams flow from the sun in filamentary structures. Birkland currents or flux tubes connect the sun to each planet through a flow of charged particles, resulting in solar flares having an almost immediate effect here are earth. While the sun was previously believed to be composed of gas, scientists like Pierre-Marie Robitaille, Ph.D., have used spectroscopy and other direct observations of the sun to clearly demonstrate the sun is composed of condensed liquid metal hydrogen. Others still, are conducting laboratory experiments replicating features of the sun in the "Safire Project".

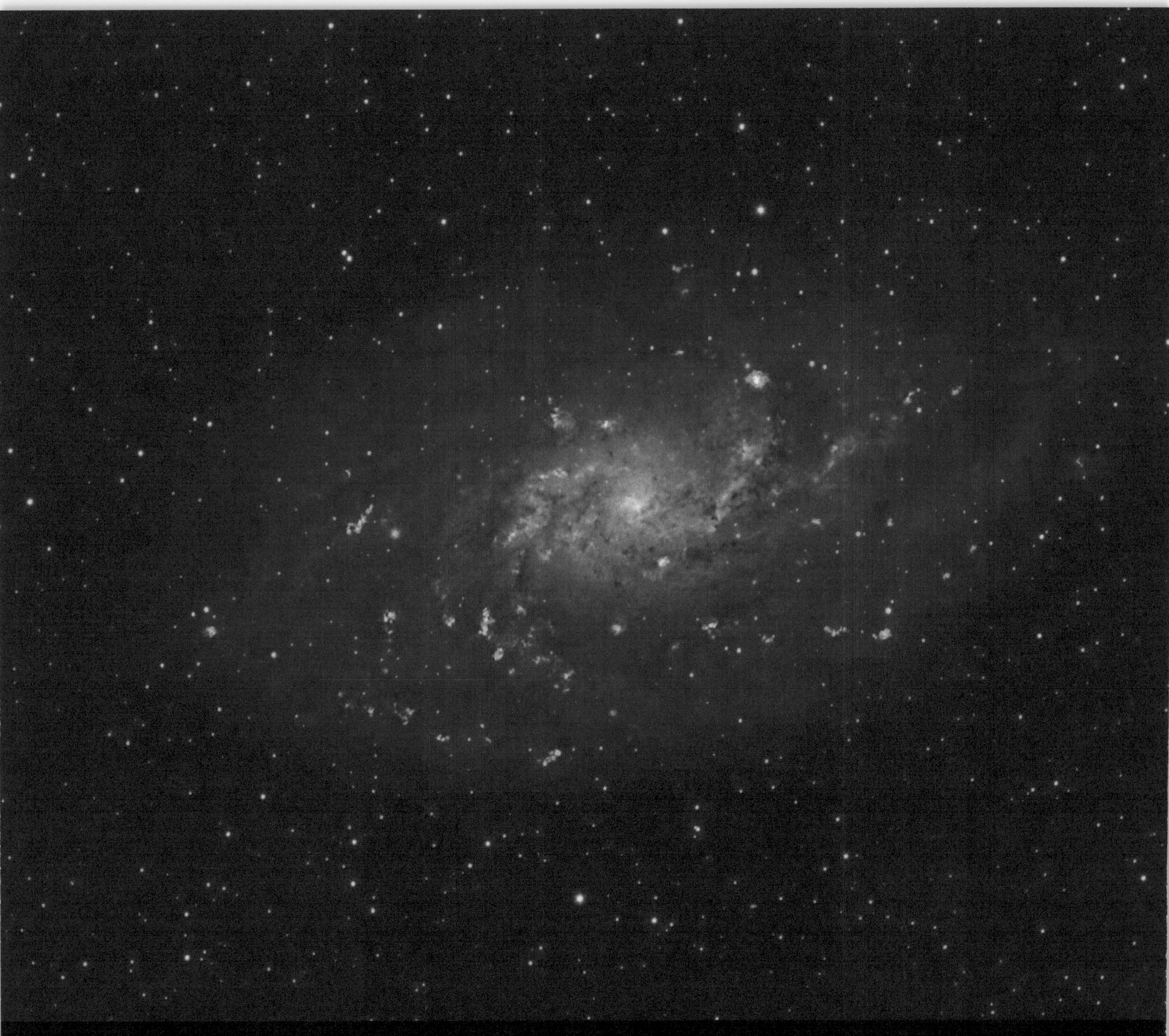

TRIANGULUM GALAXY

M33

John 1:14

The Word became flesh and made his dwelling among us. We have seen his glory, the glory of the one and only Son, who came from the Father, full of grace and truth.

Science and Thoughts

We can see in this image the numerous red and blue-green nebulas contained in the galaxy. Over 25 million stars have been resolved in the central region of the galaxy alone with an untold number of orbiting bodies. However, God chose to come to this galaxy, to a star with an orbiting body called earth, and save us.

Image Info

442 x 120 sec images total
Total integration time of 14:44 hours
Celestron SCT 6"/1500 mm 6 SCT
ZWO Optical ASI183MC Pro (CMOS)
Equatorial iOptron CEM25P
Antlia Contrast booster Quad Band
Astronomik L-1 UV-IR Blocking Filter
Focal reducer Starizona Hyperstar F2

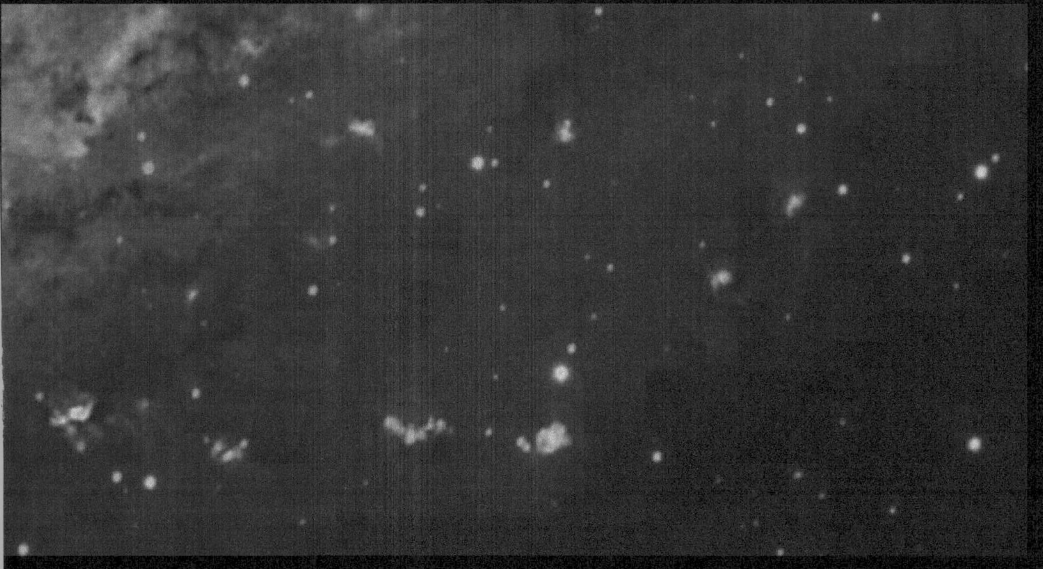

Nebulas in another Galaxy

Here we get a closer view of the blue-green (oxygen) nebulas and red (hydrogen) nebulas strewn throughout the many spiral arms of the galaxy. The distinct and reoccurring shapes of these types of nebulas is a product of the electrified nature of plasma and the electric fields that ultimately form them.

Galactic Center

With sufficient magnification, the center of the galaxy is seen with 2 arms like a bar. This is typical of plasma formations, as shown by Dr. Anthony L. Peratt, and not gravitationally driven processes. Despite the incredible detail we can obtain from space telescopes, no black hole has ever been imaged in any of these nearby galaxies. No black hole has ever been captured anywhere nor its surrounding matter.

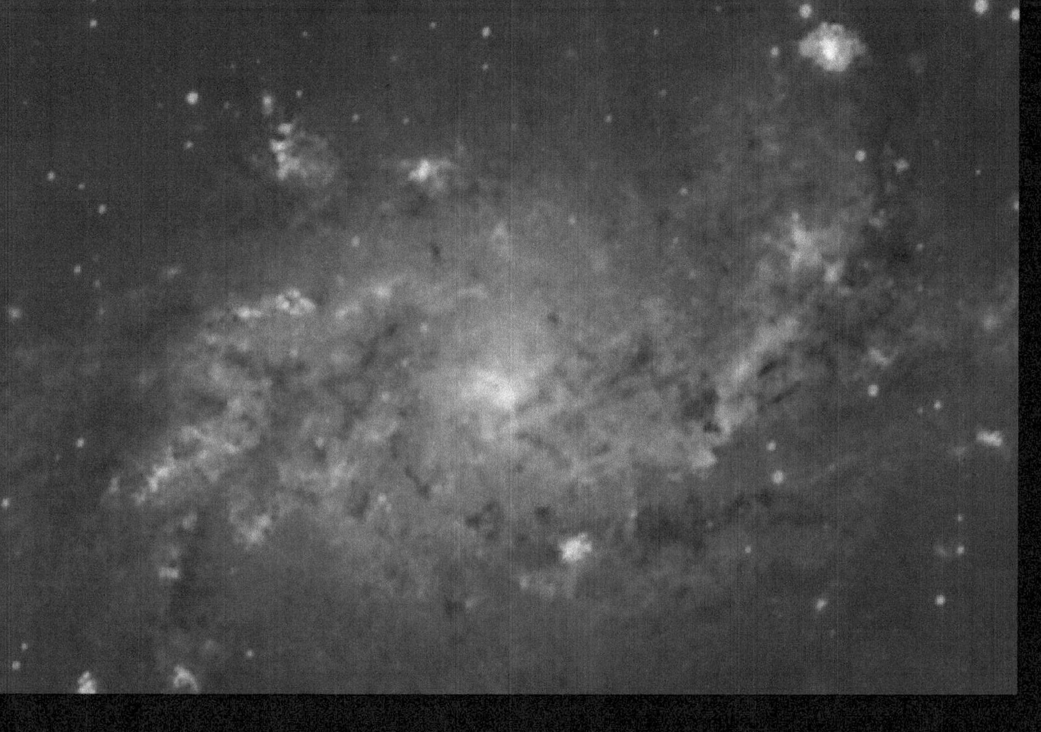

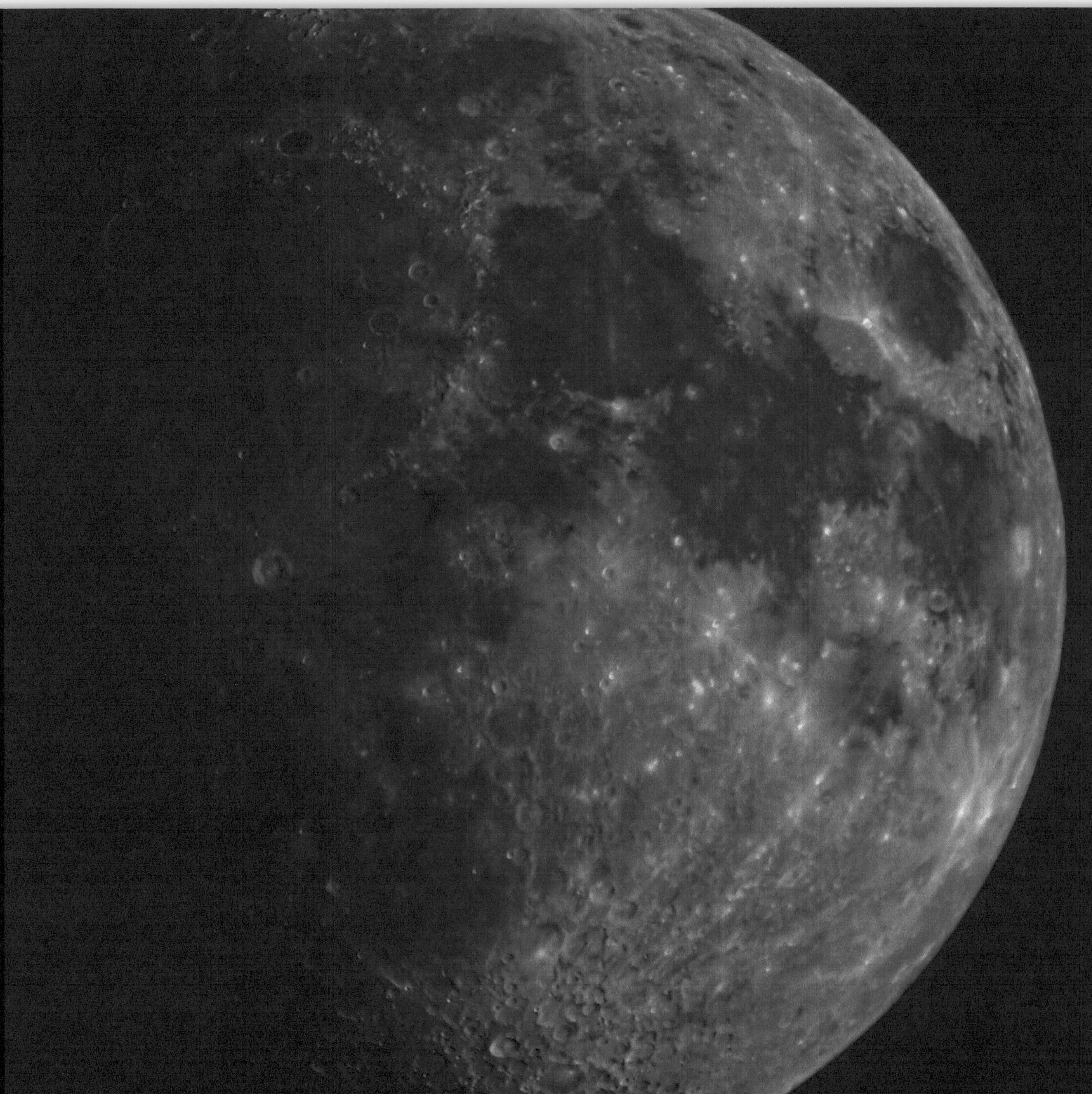

MOON

Numbers 10:10

Also, at your times of rejoicing—your appointed festivals and New Moon feasts—you are to sound the trumpets over your burnt offerings and fellowship offerings, and they will be a memorial for you before your God. I am the Lord your God.

Science and Thoughts

The moon is an average of 238,855 miles from earth and light from the moon takes 1.28 seconds to reach earth. Though it may feel far away, it is a constant companion to earth just as the Lord is a constant companion to us.

Image Info

5 images total
Meade ETX-125 SCT 5inch
Sony A6000 (CMOS) - modified
Equatorial iOptron Skyguider Pro

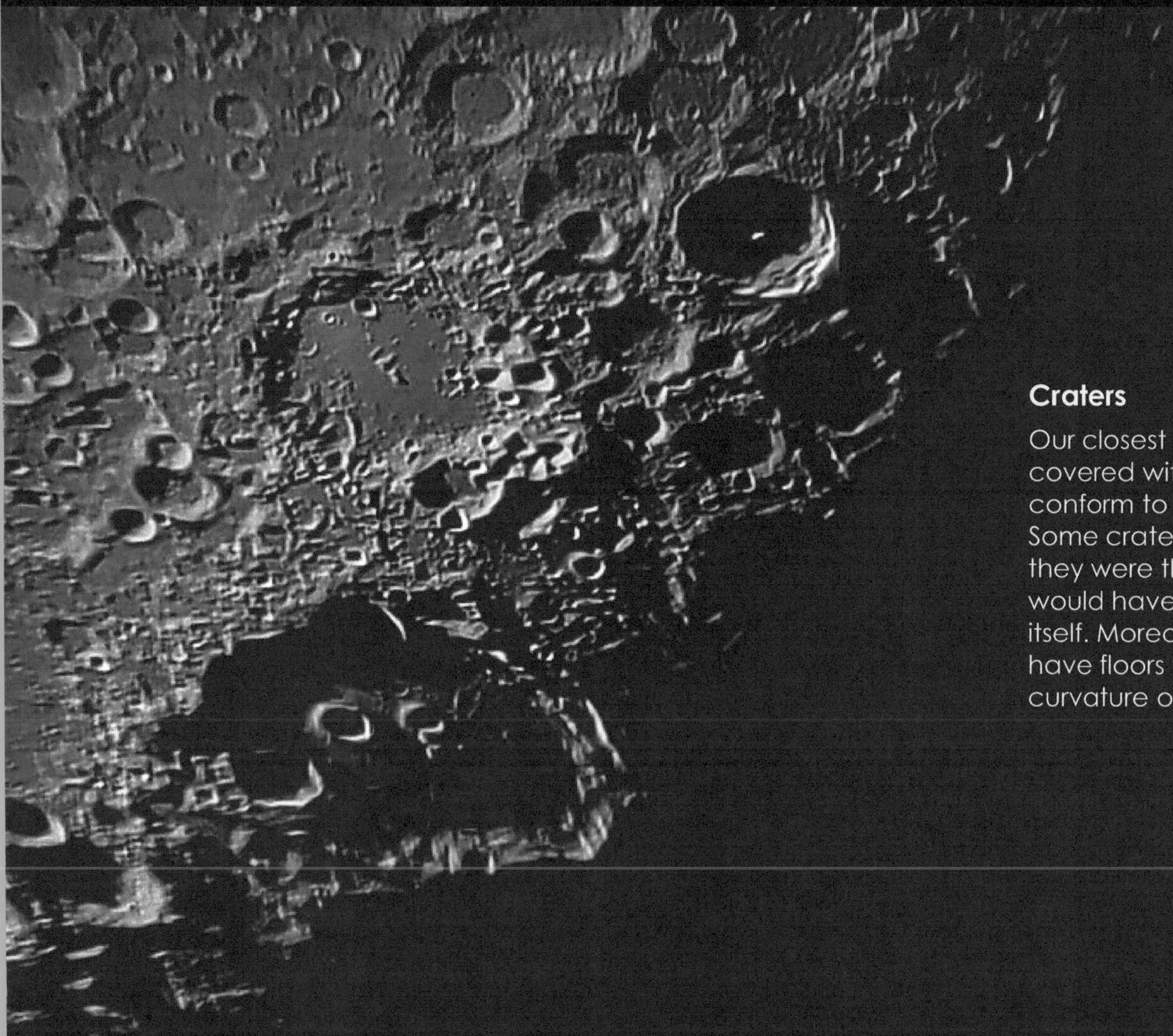

Craters

Our closest neighbor, the moon, is covered with craters that don't conform to mechanical impacts. Some craters are so large that, if they were the result of impact, would have shattered the moon itself. Moreover, these same craters have floors that conform to the curvature of the moon.

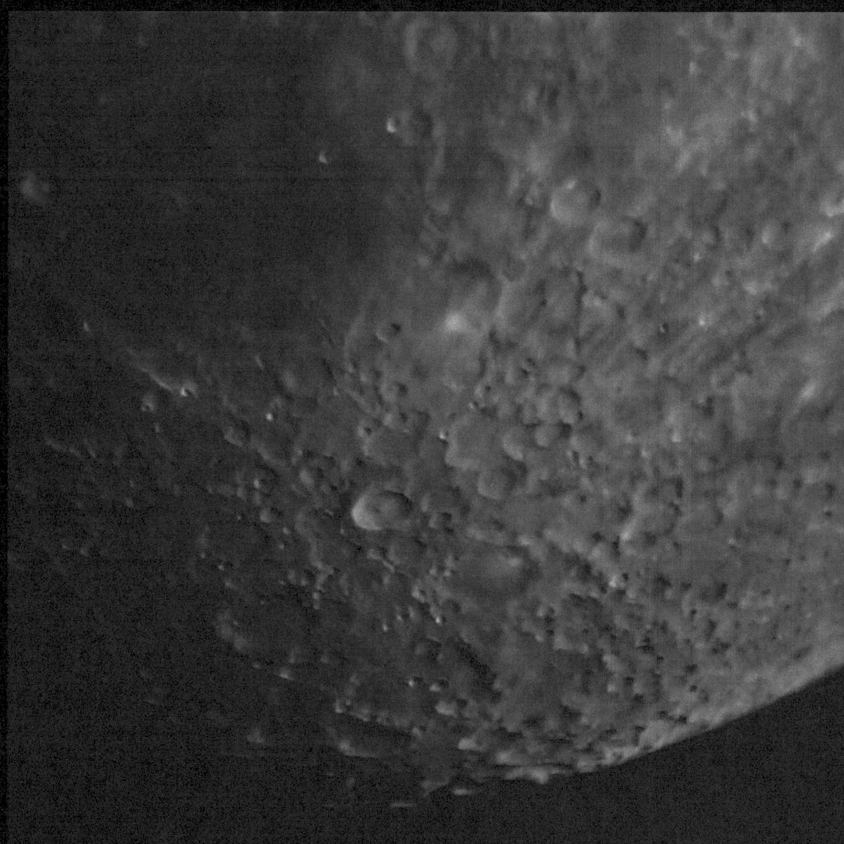

More Craters

Hexagon Craters, crater chains, raised centers, craters focused on the rims of other craters, stripes of material that would have been ejected but also converging at a point offset from the center of the associated crater.... All these have not been experimentally created by impact but have been created by electrical discharge machining.

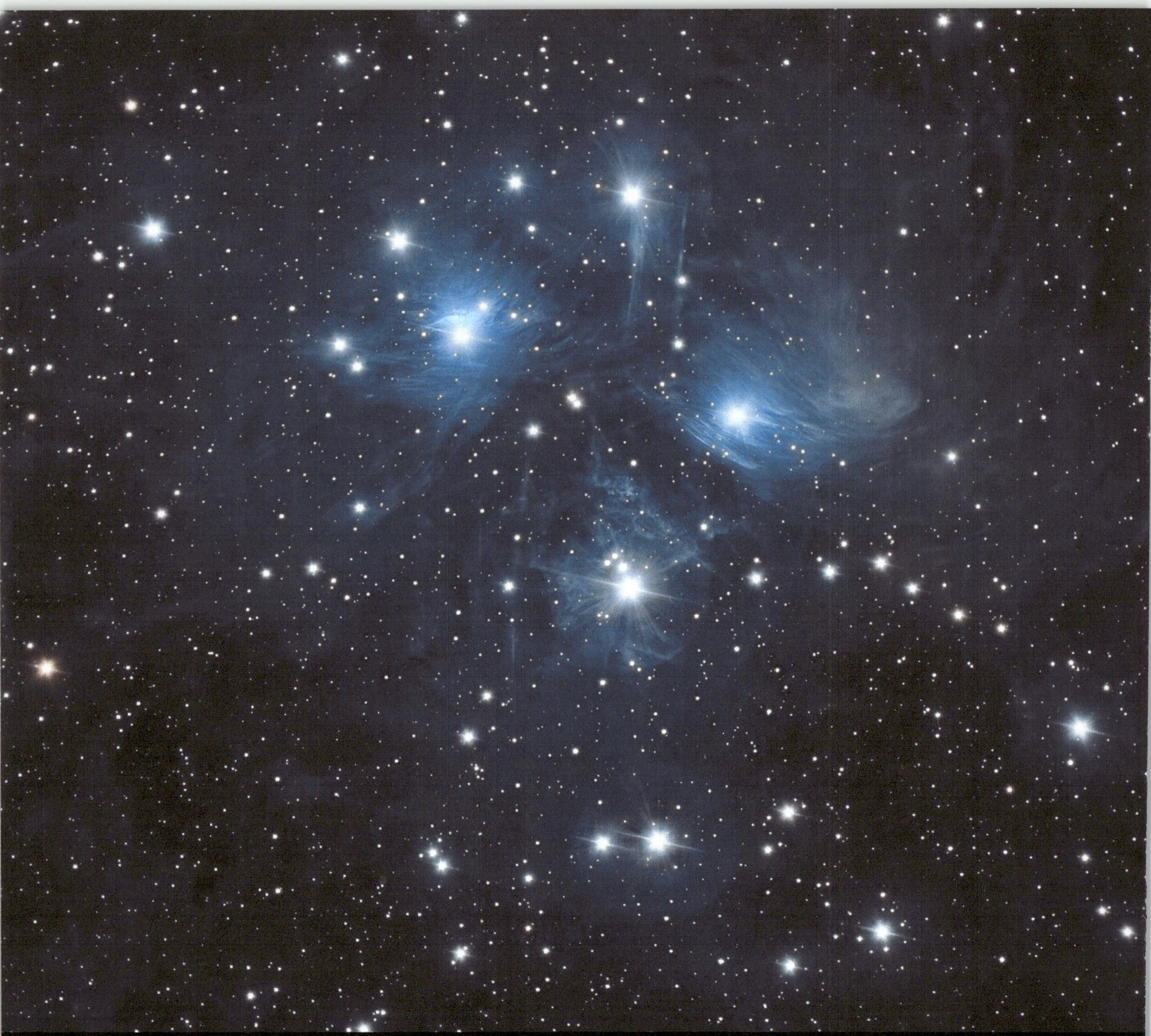

PLEIADES STAR CLUSTER

M45

Matthew 5:14

You are the light of the world. A town built on a hill cannot be hidden. Neither do people light a lamp and put it under a bowl. Instead, they put it on its stand, and it gives light to everyone in the house. In the same way, let your light shine before others, that they may see your good deeds and glorify your Father in heaven.

Science and Thoughts

This loosely grouped cluster of 1,000+ stars is orbited by our own solar system and contains dark cold gases and dust that can be seen by the reflected blue light of the bright blue stars in the cluster. The light of Christ in us should shine with the same brilliant light so that it gives light to other around us.

Image Info

493 x 60 sec images total
Total integration time of 8:13 hours
Celestron SCT 6"/1500 mm 6 SCT
ZWO Optical ASI183MC Pro (CMOS)
Equatorial iOptron CEM25P
Antlia Contrast booster Quad Band
Astronomik L-1 UV-IR Blocking Filter
Focal reducer Starizona Hyperstar F2

Strings

A common theme seen here and across the universe is a stringy or filamentary structure. In fact, recent observations has shown that our universe is organized in strings-like structures interconnecting everything. In big bang cosmology, the universe should be homogeneous, meaning evenly dispersed and dense throughout, yet we find the exact opposite. Instead the universe is strung into a tangled web of stars or galaxies grouped together. This is also expected in a universe composed of 99+ percent plasma where magnetic fields reign and charged particles flow.

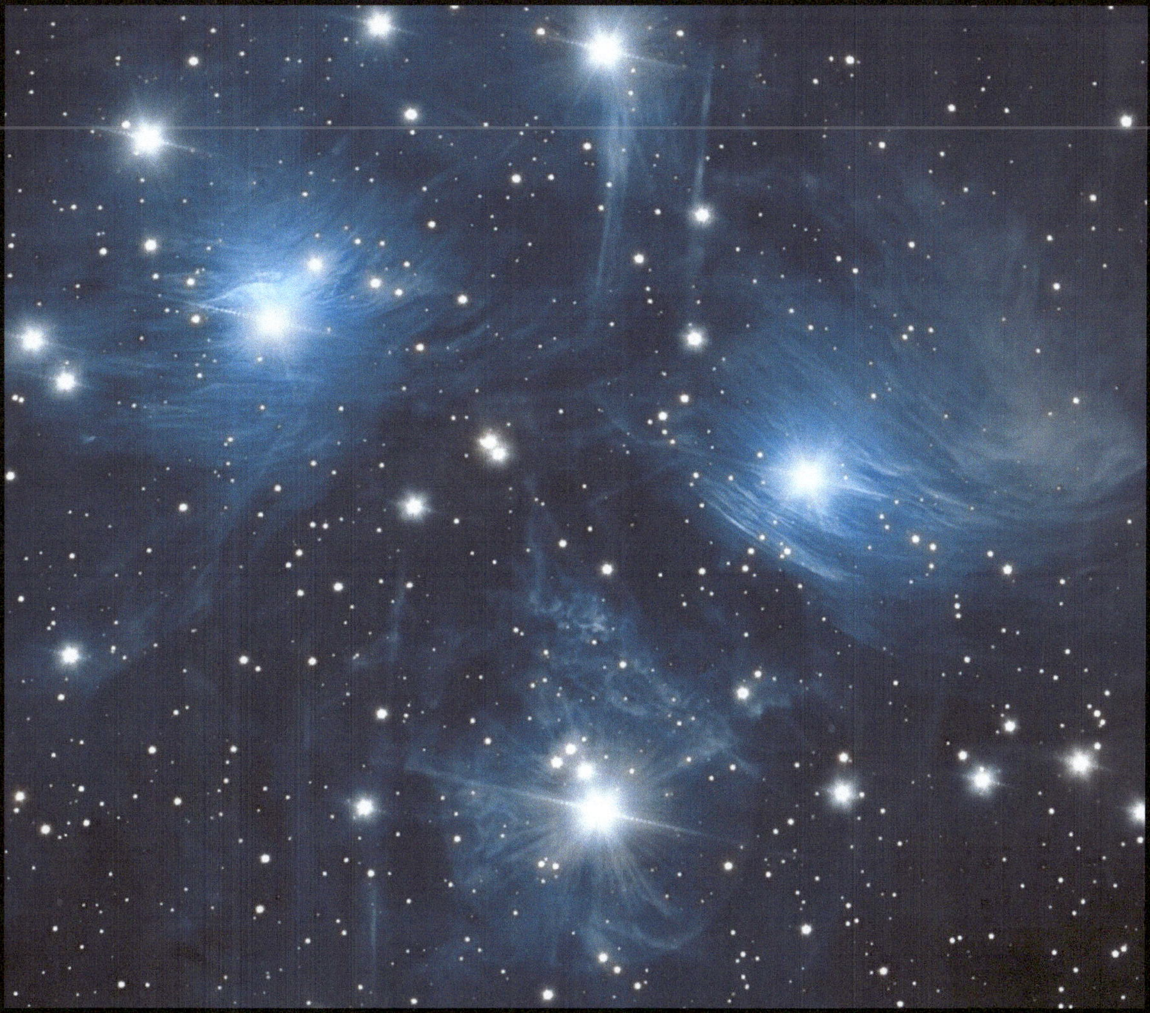

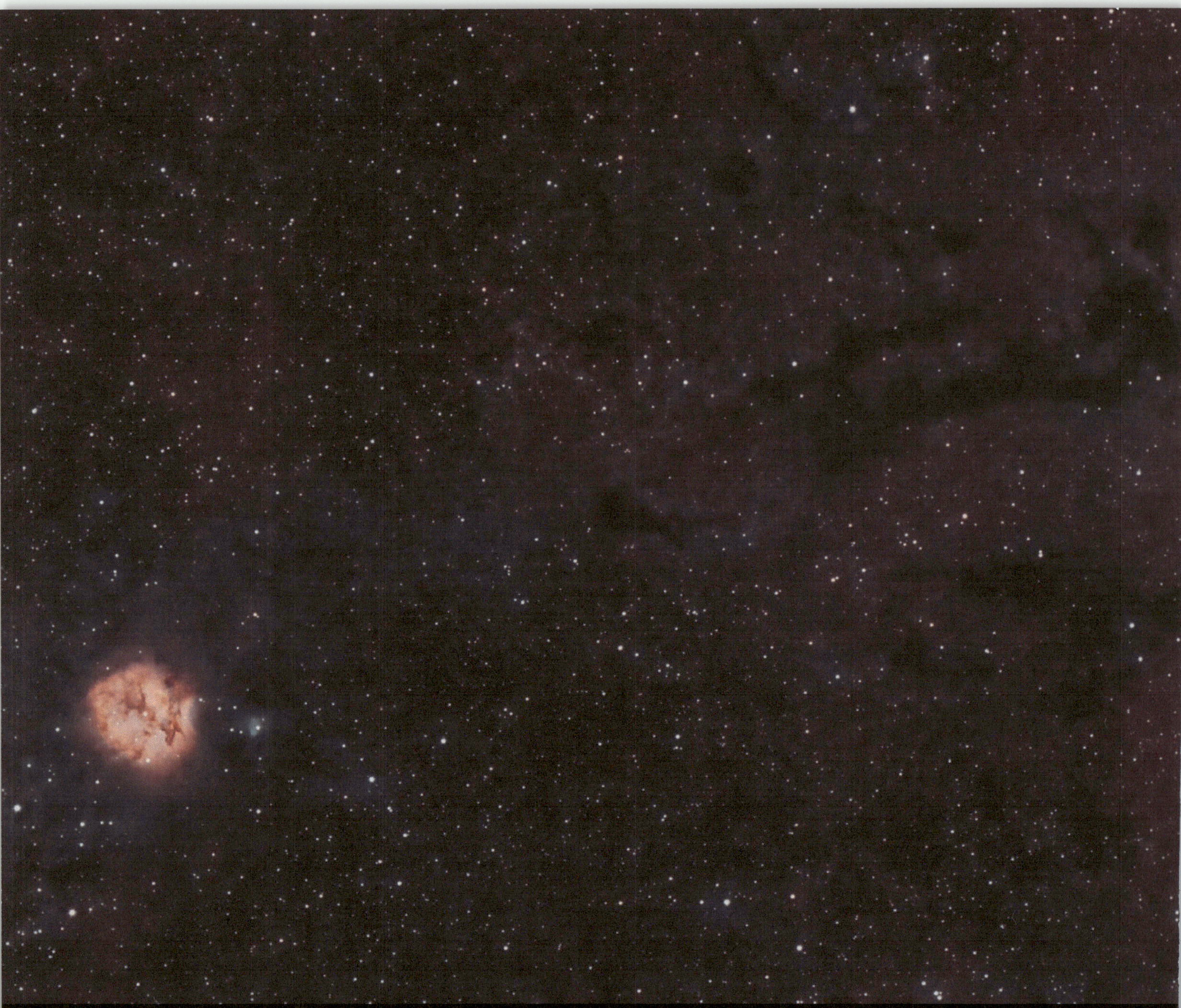

COCOON AND DARK NEBULA

IC 5146

John 17:14

I have given them your word and the world has hated them, for they are not of the world any more than I am of the world. My prayer is not that you take them out of the world but that you protect them from the evil one.

Science and Thoughts

The Cocoon nebula's plasma glows bright and alone amongst the surrounding dark nebula which is composed of cold gases and dust that is dense enough to block out the light of the stars behind it. Don't let the words darkness blot you out but let God be a cocoon of protection around you.

Image Info

415 x 120 sec images total
Total integration time of 13:50 hours
Celestron SCT 6"/1500 mm 6 SCT
ZWO Optical ASI183MC Pro (CMOS)
Equatorial iOptron CEM25P
Antlia Contrast booster Quad Band
Astronomik L-1 UV-IR Blocking Filter
Focal reducer Starizona Hyperstar F2

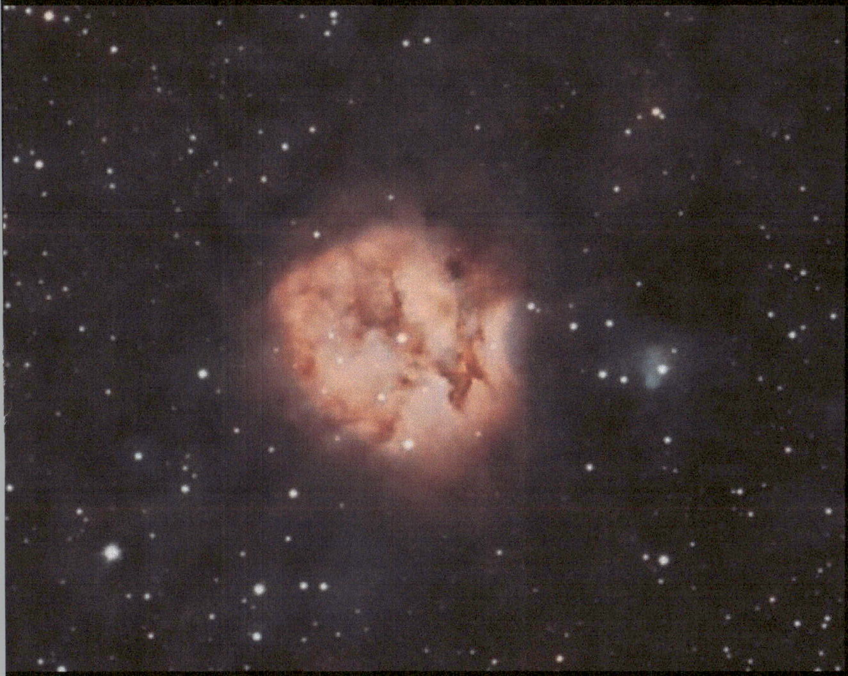

Cocoon

The red nebula is an emission nebula as the gas in the region emits its own light just like a "neon" sign. It is surrounded by gases and dust that reflects the light of nearby stars. The central star appears to be 10 to 15 times larger than our sun.

Dark Plasma

Faint grey dust and gas can be seen in the image but the dark black areas are dust and gas as well. These areas are dense enough to completely block the light from the stars behind it. Although not emitting light these dark nebulas are a plasma in "dark mode" just like the ionosphere of the earth. This is evidenced in images of different electromagnetic frequencies as collected by telescopes like the Spitzer and Chandra telescopes. For a plasma to emit in visible light spectrums, it must reach a particular energy density.

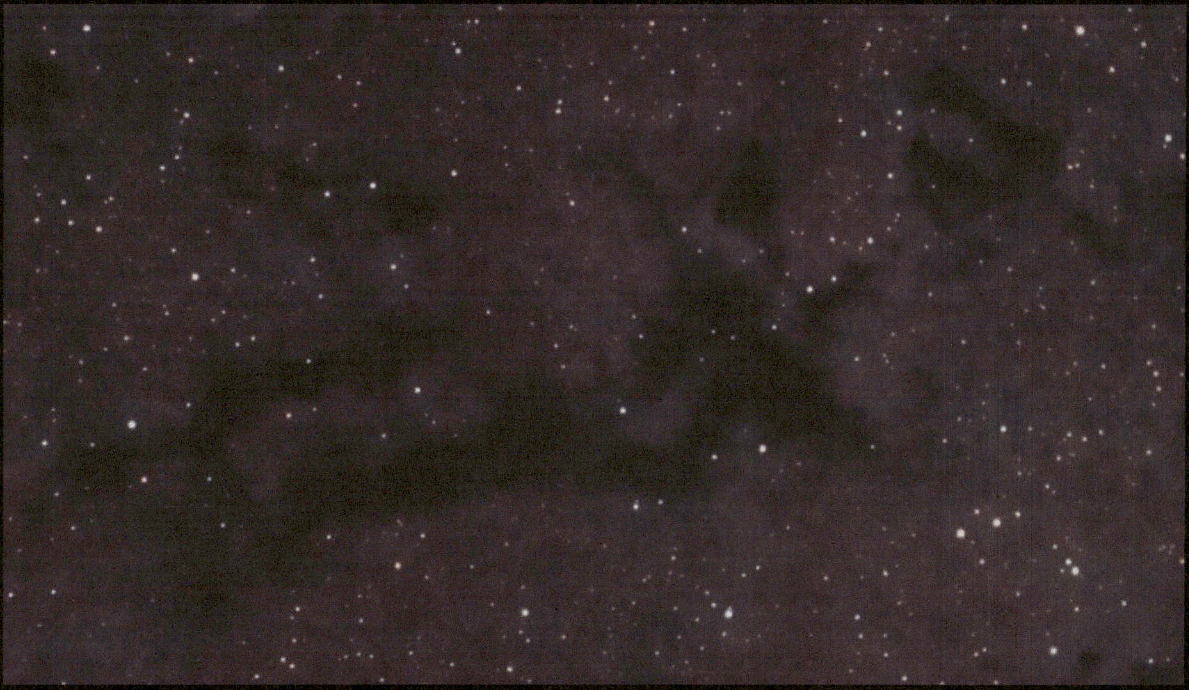

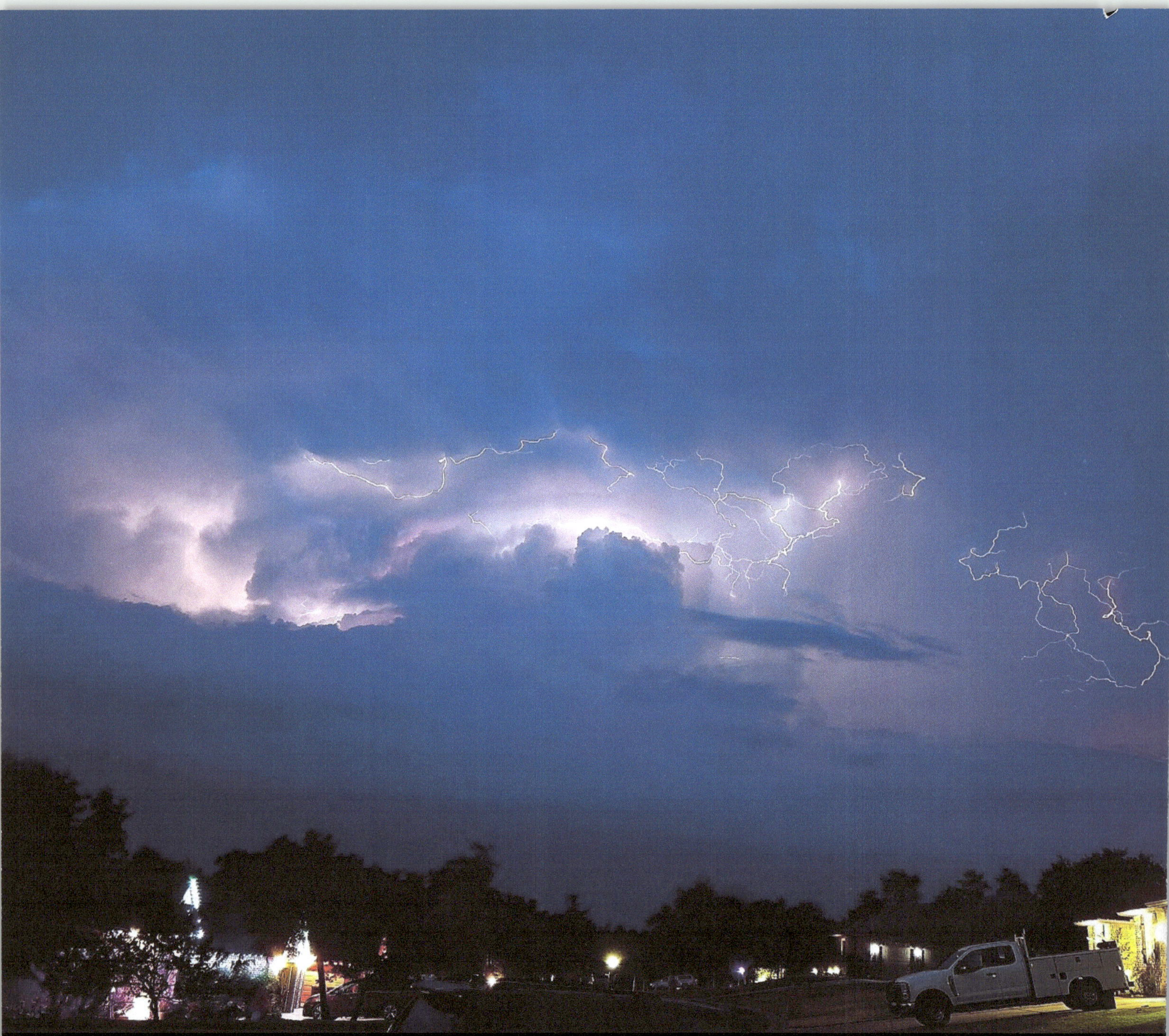

LIGHTNING STORM

Deuteronomy 9:10

The Lord gave me two stone tablets inscribed by the finger of God. On them were all the commandments the Lord proclaimed to you on the mountain out of the fire…

Science and Thoughts

99% of the universe is composed of plasma, ionized/electrified matter, and connects the universe through long twisting strands as mapped by radio and x-ray emissions. This energy feeds the sun and passes to the earth through Birkland currents (flux tubes) and collects in storms. As powerful as they appear to us they are but a miniscule fraction of the power in God's finger.

Image Info

4 x 8 sec images total
Total integration time of 0:32 minutes
Samsung Galaxy S22

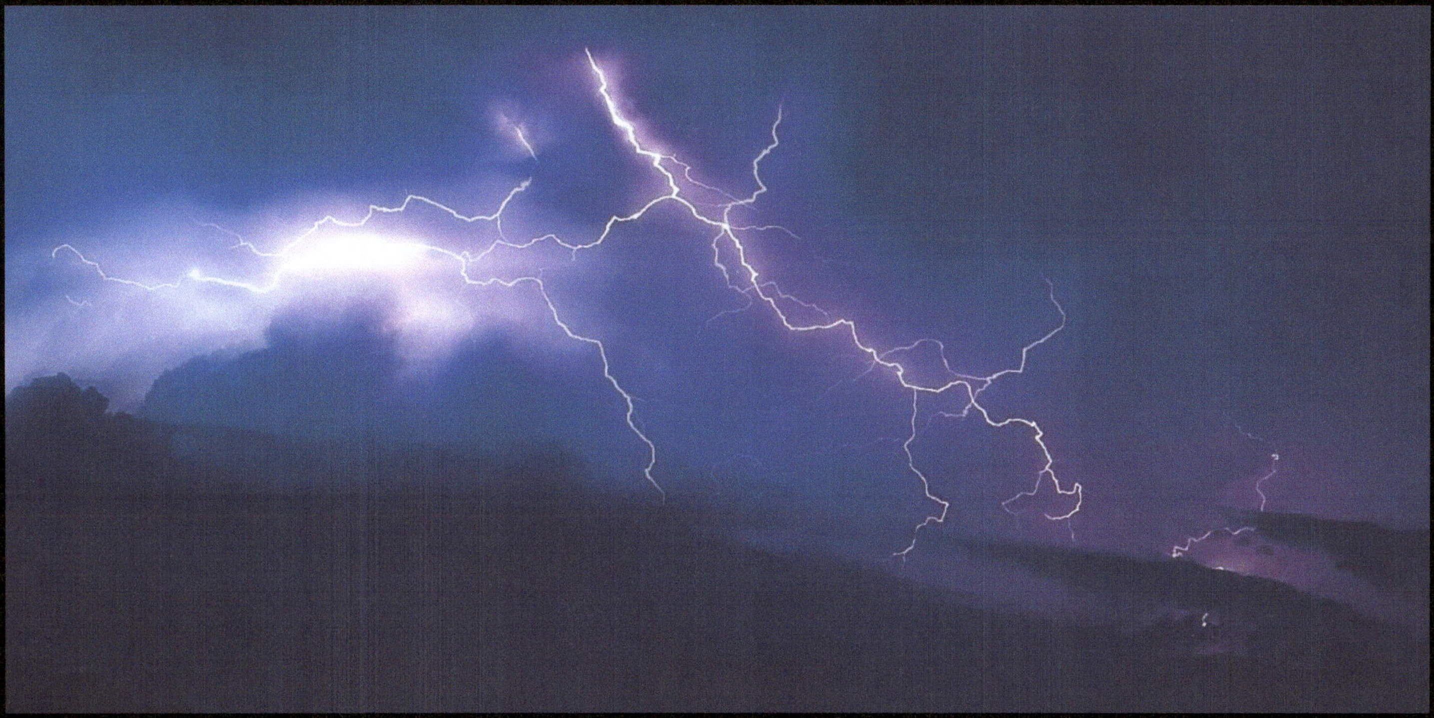

Capacitor Discharge

The mesmerizing auroras here on earth are the result of the atmosphere being energized to a plasma glow state by charged particles from the sun. Additionally, the earth's plasma double-layer, called the ionosphere, is also driven by the sun as well. The separation between the ionosphere and the earth results in a capacitor effect. However, when that insulating layer between the two is reduced or broken, discharges occur as energy flows quickly between the two seeking equilibrium.

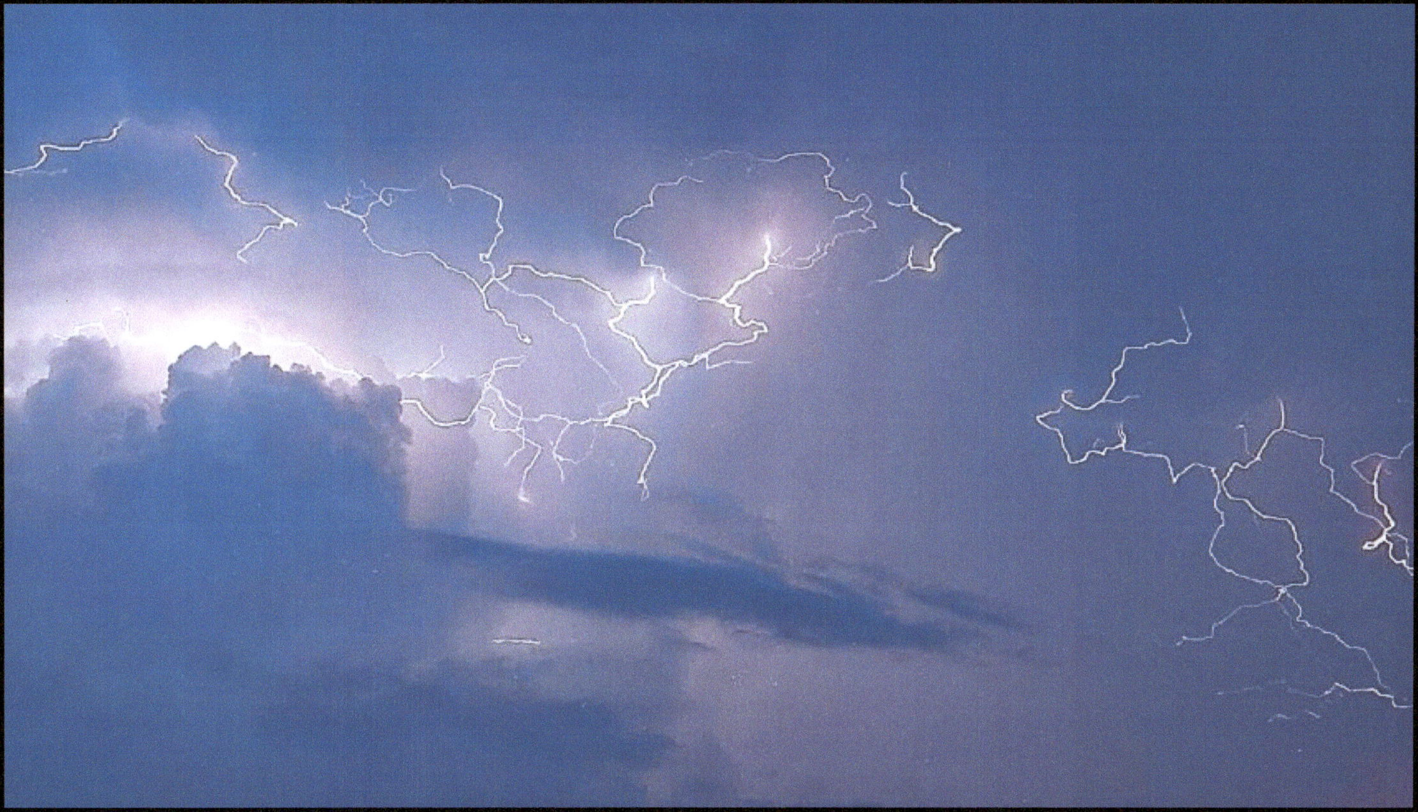

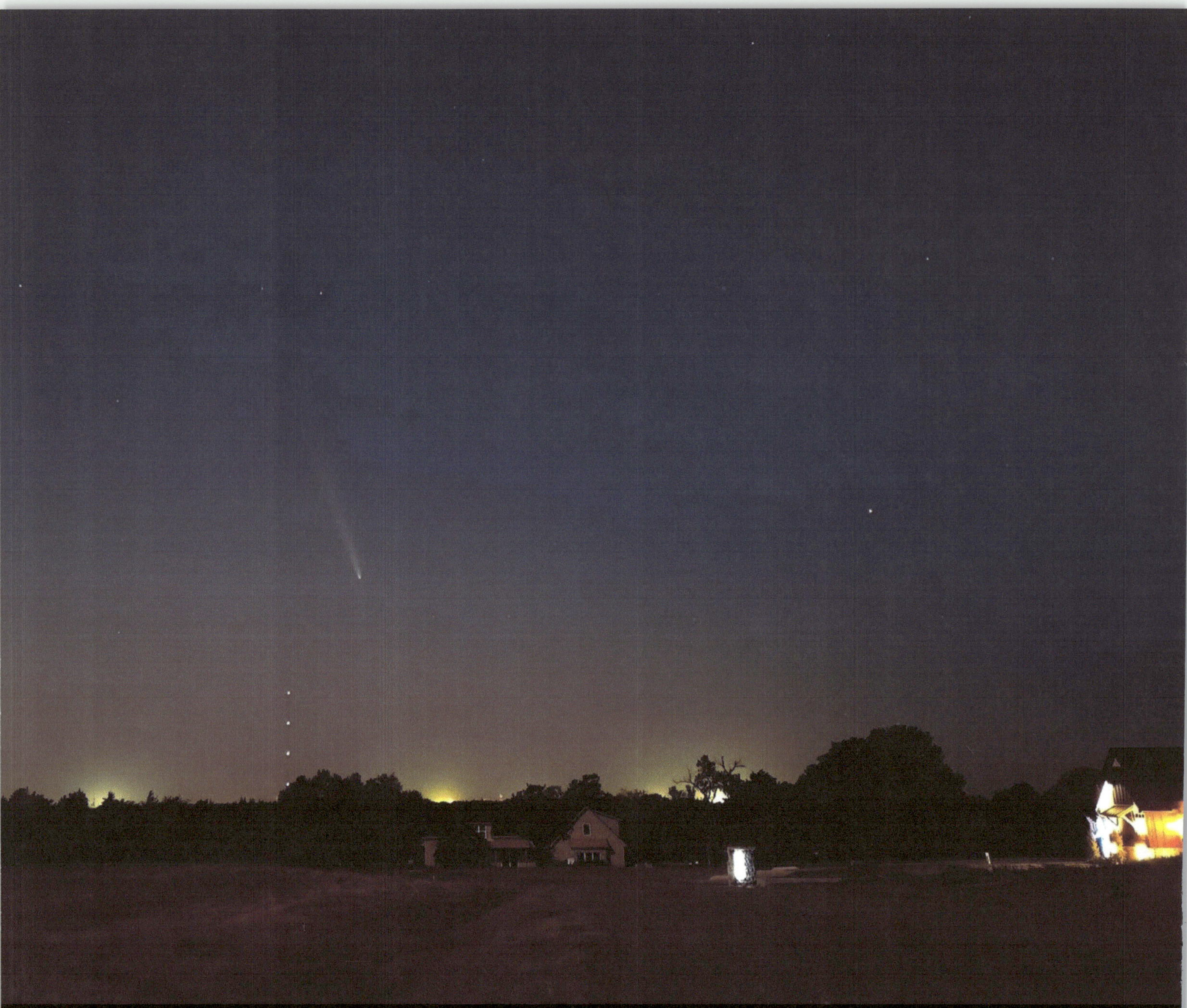

COMET C/2023 A3 TSUCHINSHAN-ATLAS

1 Corinthians 3:19

For the wisdom of this world is foolishness to God. As the Scriptures say, "He traps the wise in the snare of their own cleverness.

Science and Thoughts

Despite the never ending efforts to confirm the theory that comets are 'dirty snowballs', it fails every time. Recently, we have found that comets are being torn apart by internal electrical stress and during close passes by the sun an CME (Coronal Mass Ejection) accompanies this destruction. We must constantly remember that our trust should be in God and not the "wisdom" of this world.

Image Info

1 x 8 sec images total
Total integration time of 2:00 minutes
Samsung Galaxy S22

Dirty Snowball?

The standard accepted theory of comets is that they are dirty snowballs, yet they have continually exhibited features and behaviors contrary to the that explanation. In July of 2005 the "Deep Impact" mission shot a projectile at a comet. Wallace Thornhill and his colleagues made a large number of predictions that were in conflict with dirty snowball theory. Thornhill's predictions included things like no water being found on the comet or released by the impact, a bright flash of light before the impact, the effect will exceed that of a physical impact, new collimated filamentary jets on parts other than the impact location, and others. While NASA and dirty snowball advocates were stunned and baffled with the many successful predictions of Thornhill and his colleagues, and the failures of their predictions, consensus 'science' has yet to abandon the dirty snowball theory.

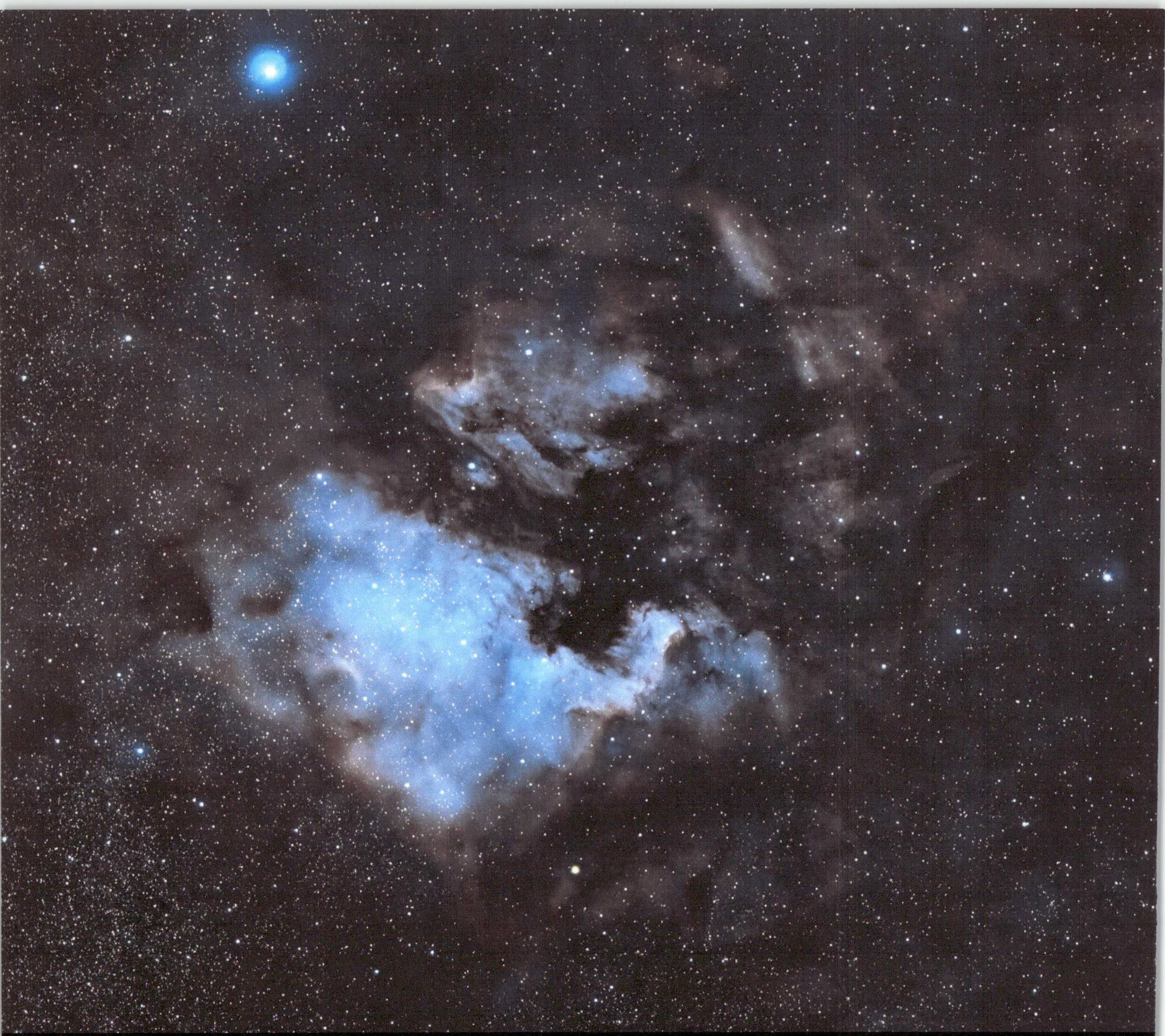

NORTH AMERICAN NEBULA
NGC 7000

Isaiah 52:7

How lovely on the mountains
Are the feet of him who brings good news,
Who announces peace
And brings good news of happiness,
Who announces salvation,
And says to Zion, "Your God reigns!

Science and Thoughts

Using triangulation, this nebula of hydrogen and oxygen is approximately 2,590 light years away and located in our own galaxy. For those who dedicate the time and search the sky, there is great reward in the finding and capturing of such beauty. Those who dedicate themselves to seeking God obtain the most beautiful and greatest reward.

Image Info

58 x 60 sec images total
Total integration time of 0:58 hours
Rokinon Lens 135 mm F2
Sony A6000 (CMOS) - modified
Equatorial iOptron Skyguider Pro
SVBONY Broadband UHC Filter
(False Color - Red=Ha Blue=OIII)

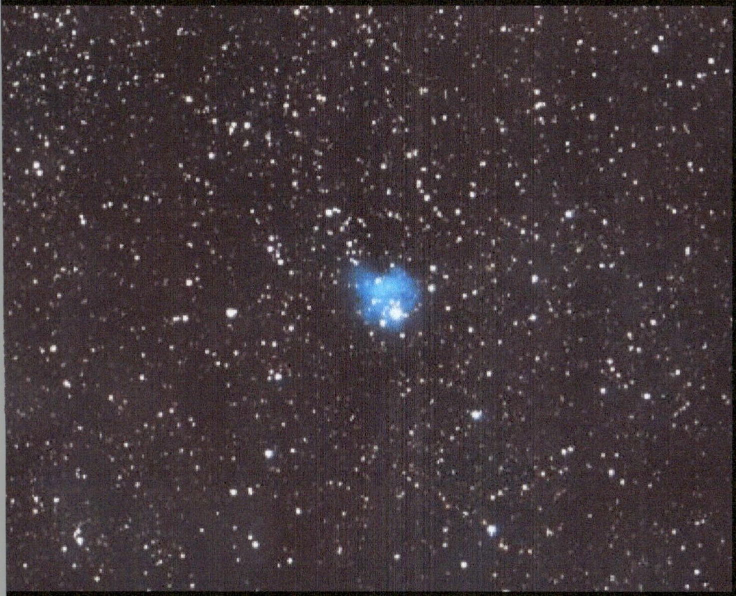

IC 5076

In the upper left of the original image (cropped off due to the page size) a small reflection nebula is found. The blue star that is illuminating the nebula fluctuates in brightness by 0.1 magnitudes over the course of 27 to 55 days.

One Molecular Cloud

Though originally cataloged as two separate nebulas (the North American in the lower left and Pelican in the upper right) it is actually a single molecular cloud separate by bands of dark gas and dust. From our perspective it appears to cover 10 times the area of the full moon. The star believed by some to be lighting the nebula is not hot enough to do so. This is most likely due to the fact that nebulas are not being energized by ionizing radiation from nearby stars but from the flow of charge through the galactic medium.

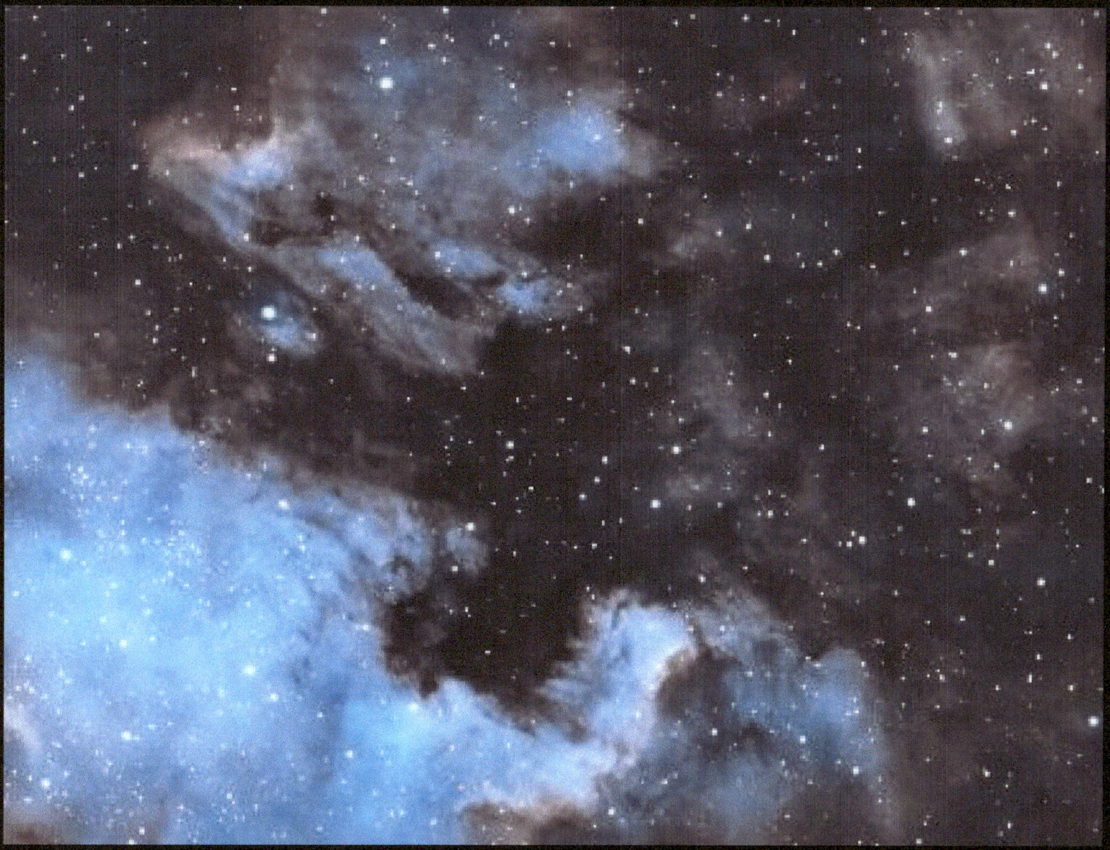

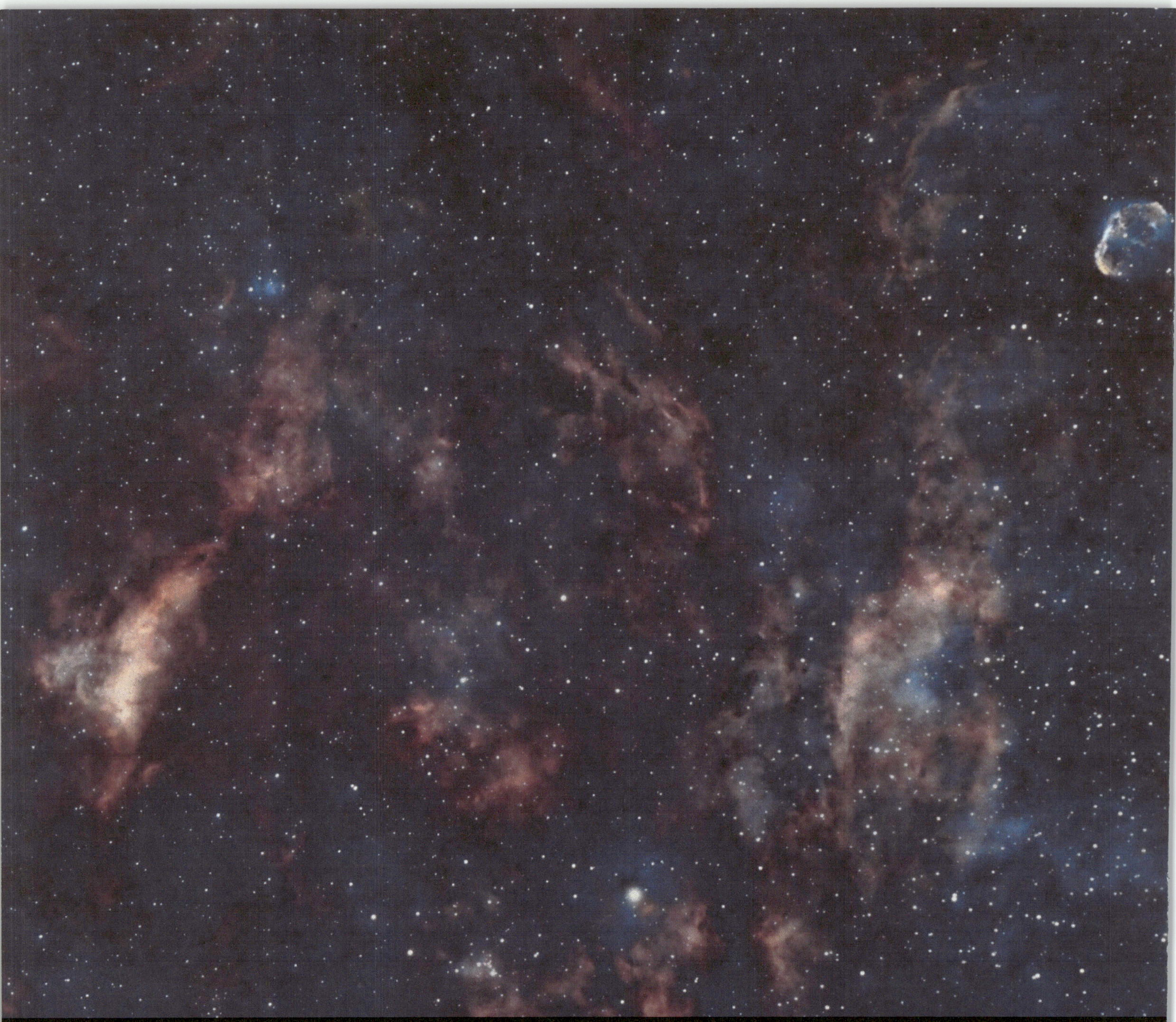

SADR REGION

IC 1318,
SH 2-108,
NGC 6888,
LBN 222,
LDN 895, ETC.

1 Corinthians 15:58

Therefore, my dear brothers and sisters, stand firm. Let nothing move you. Always give yourselves fully to the work of the Lord, because you know that your labor in the Lord is not in vain.

Science and Thoughts

This area of the sky is full of plasma and energy in a dense and active region of our Milky Way galaxy. SADR stands large and strong as brightest star in the lower center of the image with a radius 150 time larger than our sun's radius. Stand strong in the turmoil of this life like this star.

Image Info

78 x 90 sec & 16 x 60 sec images total
Total integration time of 2:13 hours
Rokinon 135mm F2
ZWO Optical ASI183MC Pro (CMOS)
Equatorial iOptron CEM25P
Antlia Contrast booster Quad Band
Astronomik L-1 UV-IR Blocking Filter

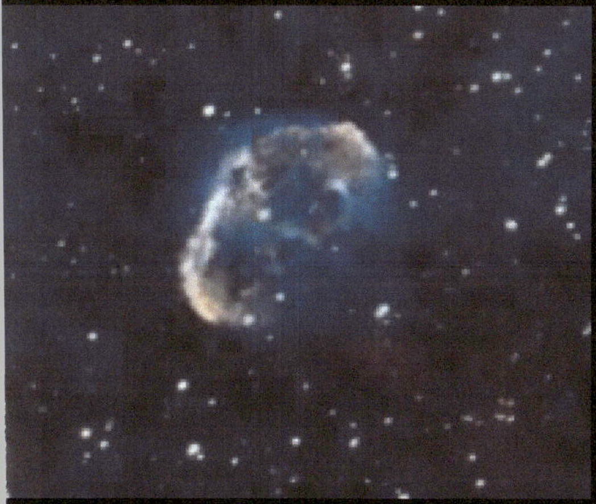
Cresent Nebula NGC 6888

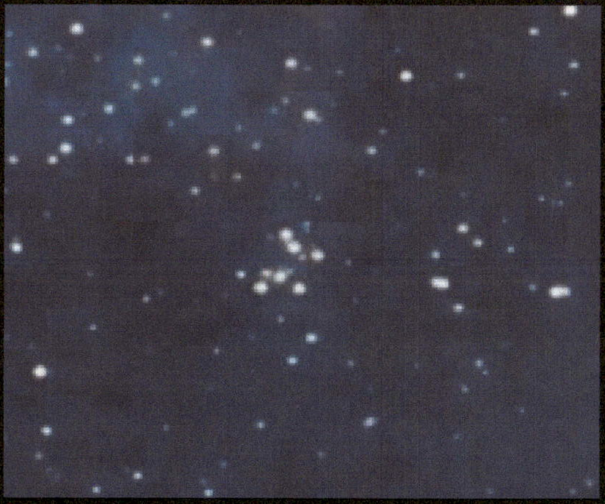
Cooling Tower Cluster M29

This area of the sky is full of objects. star clusters, emission nebulas, dark nebulas, etc.

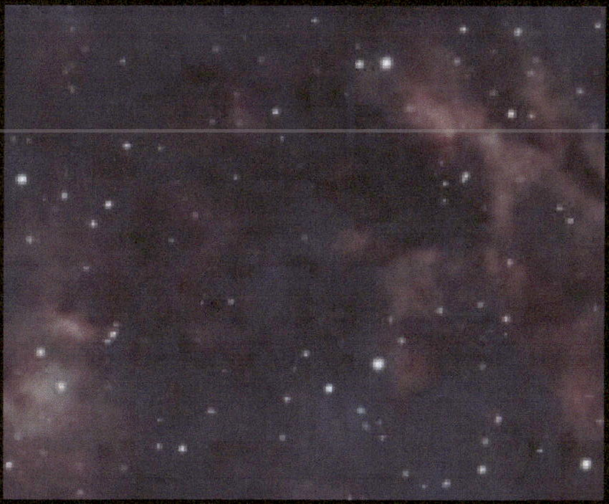
Dark Nebula BARNARD 343

Star Cluster 6910

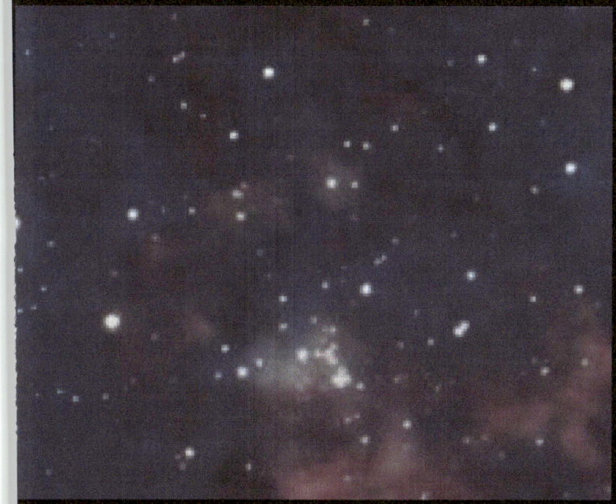

Emission Nebula IC 1318A

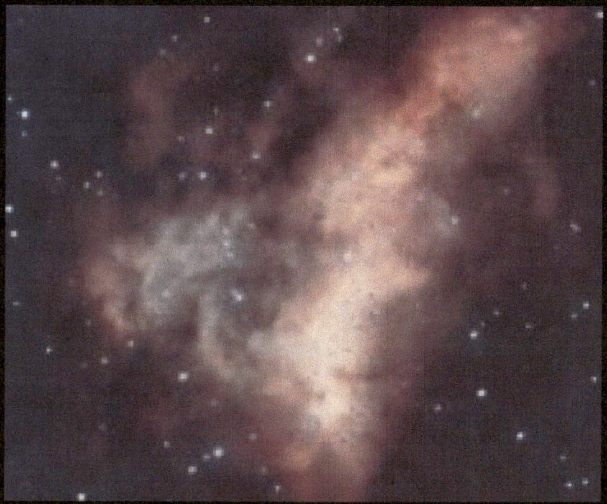

www.ingramcontent.com/pod-product-compliance
Lightning Source LLC
Chambersburg PA
CBHW051838210526
45473CB00005B/1932
* 9 7 9 8 3 0 3 5 3 9 8 6 0 *